PRAISE FOR THE EMPLOYEE-CENTRIC MANAGER

"When you understand and nurture what employees want and need to succeed, you create a powerful competitive advantage. Dr. Wiley's book mirrors the values our company holds dear. That's why I ordered copies for every manager in our organization."

John Dreyer, President and CEO, The Shelby Group

"As organisations face awe-inspiring rates of change, having highly effective managers becomes ever more central to organisational success. Jack Wiley brings his extensive and in-depth experience to bear in offering practical approaches and inspiring examples of how to apply the eight keys to managerial success."

David MacLeod, Co-Founder, Engage for Success
Co-Author, The MacLeod Report to the UK Government on Employee Engagement

"Creating a great career experience for your people starts with the manager. Dr. Jack's book gives every manager real-life examples and actionable insights to turn each interaction into better business results."

Phil Stewart, CEO, Engage2Excel

THE EMPLOYEE-CENTRIC MANAGER

I dedicate this book to my children –
Nathan, Luke, Megan, and Jackson.

THE EMPLOYEE-CENTRIC MANAGER

8 Keys to People-Management Effectiveness

Dr. Jack Wiley

www.EmployeeCentricity.com

Published by Employee Centiricty LLC, La Fontaine, Indiana.

Library of Congress Cataloging-in Publication Data

Wiley, Jack

The Employee-Centric Manager: 8 keys to people-management effectiveness / Jack Wiley—1st ed.

p. cm

Includes bibliographic references AND INDEX.

ISBN: 978-0-578-92037-5

Printed in the United States of America

FIRST EDITION

Acknowledgments

In the research and writing of this book, I am indebted to several colleagues. The original research team that explored the fundamental question of what employees most want from their immediate manager included Brenda Kowske, Rena Rasch, and Haiyan Zhang. Rena and Haiyan were instrumental in overseeing the analysis of the global qualitative data and producing the eight-attribute taxonomy.

In more recent years, other research associates contributed to the development of methods for measuring the managerial display of the eight attributes and the calibration of their influence on important employee and team outcomes. Chief among those associates are former students Veronica Caudill and Connor Eichenauer. Veronica also oversaw the collection of the critical incidents data and, along with Meghan McClimon, analyzed this qualitative dataset.

Executives for Engage2Excel provided substantial organizational support and investment for critical stages of this ongoing research program. Special recognition is due Phil Stewart, Jeff Gelinas, and Melissa Meunier. Jeff has been an ongoing source of support and guidance throughout all stages of the writing of this book.

Special recognition is due to Mark Felton. Not only did Mark encourage me to write this book and bring forth the message about what employees most want from their managers, he also contributed the eight profiles of employee-centric managers. In addition, Mark and his colleagues at Signal Marketing guided and helped with all stages of book design and production. Their contributions have been invaluable.

In truth, many have contributed to the development of this book and the program of research upon which it is based. Not the least of which are the over 80,000 employees whose voices have spoken. I trust my summary of what they had to say is accurate, truthful, and helpful.

Contents

List of Figures and Tables

Foreword

People-management skills have a profound influence on employee engagement, performance, and retention. However, if you are like most managers, you've probably received little or no training in people management. Not surprisingly, recent surveys from a variety of professional sources have catalogued the lost productivity and worker stress resulting from poorly trained managers.

Over the course of my career as a professor, researcher, and consultant to management I have read countless articles, white papers, and books on the role of the manager in the modern workplace. But I have yet to come across a comprehensive guide to improving day-to-day people-management skills written expressly for managers.

Jack Wiley is just the person to fill this void. For the past 35 years of his career, Jack has been focused on getting answers to questions about what employees really want from their employers, CEOs, coworkers, and immediate bosses. He chose a novel path for generating these answers—he simply asked employees directly. Oddly, this had never been done before. His first book from this stream of research was entitled *RESPECT, Delivering Results by Giving Employees What They Really Want. RESPECT* answered the question of what employees most want from the organizations for which they work and showed how organizations who provide a superior employee experience enjoy higher levels of customer satisfaction and greater financial returns.

In *The Employee-Centric Manager*, Jack follows the same path by asking over 80,000 employees worldwide this simple question:

"What is the most important thing you want from your immediate manager?" The analysis of this resulting mass of data produced a framework of eight attributes employees most frequently identify as their "wants" in a manager. But Jack did not stop there. In this book he also shows how being the kind of manager employees prefer connects to higher levels of employee engagement and enhanced team productivity.

Jack has masterfully converted the simplicity of his findings into useful advice he offers to managers and leaders. This book provides thoughtful, practical, and easy-to-implement actions that managers and leaders can take right now to boost managerial effectiveness and improve employee productivity and retention. If you are a manager or leader who is interested in improving your effectiveness and your employees' work experience, you have picked up the right book.

Charles A. Scherbaum, PhD
Professor of Industrial and Organizational Psychology
Department of Psychology
Baruch College, City University of New York

Introduction

If your job involves managing others, this book is for you.

It doesn't matter if you have only one employee or manage a team of 10, a department of 30, or a division of 100 employees. It doesn't matter if you manage a Fortune 500 company, a small multi-generational family business, or a start-up. If you have people-management responsibilities, this book is written with you in mind.

Let's start by reviewing **your** goals. If you are like other managers, your goals likely include the following:

- You want to get along well with the members of your team.
- You want your team members to get along well with each other.
- You want your team or workforce to be highly engaged.
- You want your team or workforce to operate at the highest levels of performance.
- Personally, you want to achieve the best possible performance reviews.
- Personally, you want to maximize your rewards.

Let's think about this. Isn't it logical that becoming a better people manager is one of the surest pathways to achieving these goals? If you agree, let me ask you another question: ***Do you know how to become a better people manager?***

At the heart of this book is a simple truth: Becoming a better people manager begins with knowledge. In this book, I lay out for you all I have learned about what the best people managers look like. I show you the type of manager employees prefer, the type of manager employees would design or build ... if only they were asked.

The truth of the matter is that I **have** asked this question. In fact, I have asked it to over 80,000 employees in 27 countries around the world, and this book reveals what they told me. It boils down to this: Employees want managers who display ***eight fundamental attributes.*** What employees most want in their managers is that they ...

1. **Show support and consideration**
2. **Provide recognition**
3. **Treat employees with dignity and respect**
4. **Communicate clear performance expectations**
5. **Reward performance contributions by ensuring fair pay and providing developmental opportunities**
6. **Demonstrate competence in problem-solving and decision-making**
7. **Are just and fair**
8. **Are honest and trustworthy**

That's it. These are the eight attributes that employees said they most wanted in their managers. These eight attributes define the *employee-centric manager.*

None of these desired attributes is particularly hard to understand. The first five refer to behaviors. In this context, these behaviors are actions managers use to adjust to and influence their employees. The sixth attribute is a skill, and skills pertain to how well you do something; a skill is developed through practice. The final two attributes are values, which are standards of behavior. The values you display reveal what is truly important to you.

As a total package, this is the ***5-1-2 theory of managerial effectiveness.*** The theory starts with these five behaviors, one skill, and two values. But a theory is merely a way of organizing ideas to *explain an outcome*. In this case, the theory states that managers who demonstrate the 5-1-2 attributes are more likely to get along well with their employees and their team members are more likely to get along well with each other. In addition, these managers' teams are more highly engaged in their work and operate at higher levels of performance. These managers achieve superior performance reviews and maximize their rewards. In other words, employee-centric managers are by far most likely to achieve their goals.

Do you want to increase the probability of achieving your goals? If so, this book is written for you. It details the eight attributes employees want in their managers and what a manager can do to become or improve as an employee-centric manager. You learn about the dos and don'ts of each attribute and the actions you can take to enhance your performance. You will see how the 5-1-2 theory works and the evidence that supports it. Along the way, I share with you this reality: Most managers overestimate how well they perform as an employee-centric manager. In the eyes of their employees, they are notably less employee-centric than their self-estimate. That creates a perception-performance gap. The manager who is willing to improve, the one who wants to close that gap is the manager that this book targets. That manager attracts and retains the very best employees and oversees a high-performance team. That manager gets the best performance reviews, the best pay, and the best opportunities for job growth and career development. Is that you?

CHAPTER 1

Nine Reasons You Should Read This Book

I've spent the past four decades researching human dynamics in the workplace. But this is not a book about research. It's a book about you and how you can become a better people manager—one that employees really want to work for. The recommendations in this book will help you attract and retain employees who are willing to go above and beyond what is expected of them. These recommendations will help you improve the productivity of the teams you manage, increase your managerial effectiveness ratings, and help you earn promotions and higher pay.

Here are nine reasons you should read this book, digest its contents, and apply its lessons. Every one of these reasons is supported by research that I briefly refer to here. If you want to dig deeper into the research that supports these nine reasons, you'll find it in appendix 3.

1. You want to better understand what employees want most from you.

As a manager, you no doubt want to take pride in the relationships you develop with employees. But let's face it, many employees are often reluctant to share what they really think with their manager. I asked 1,000 people managers this question: "As a people manager, what do you believe is the most important thing your employees want from you?" I then compared their responses to what employees said they most wanted from their manager. The results are in Table 1.1.

Table 1.1

The Employee – Manager (Dis)Connection*

Managerial Attributes	What Employees Want	What Managers Think Employees Want**	Close Match?
Support and Understanding	25%	16%	No
Recognition	13%	1%	No
Dignity and Respect	13%	10%	Yes
Clear Performance Expectations	17%	15%	Yes
Reward Performance Contributions	7%	5%	Yes
Problem-Solving and Decision-Making	12%	19%	No
Fair and Just	8%	5%	No
Honest and Trustworthy	5%	13%	No

*Data based on samples from the United States
**Column totals to less than 100% because 16% of managers identified Overall Management and Leadership Skills as what employees most wanted from them

Let's focus on the attributes of support and understanding and recognition, the two attributes with the biggest employee-manager preference gaps. What do you see? Managers underestimate by a sizable degree how important it is for them to support, understand, and recognize the members of their teams. As logical people, we act based on the information we have. But by how much do we underperform when our information is faulty, or our knowledge is limited?

Later in the book, I explain what employees mean when they say they want your support and understanding, and your recognition. Knowing these things will increase your awareness. But that's only the first step: The real test is what you do with your increased awareness. Keep reading.

2. You want to become a top-notch people manager.

As a manager, you have an appreciation for the value of training, right? Training is about—or should be about—gaining knowledge, acquiring skills, changing behavior, and improving performance. But how much training have you received in improving your capabilities as a people manager? If your answer is not enough, you're not alone.

A recent survey I conducted indicates that *over 70% of managers have either received no people-management training at all or received only four hours.* (See Figure 1.1) Given the outsized importance of the *people-management* component of a manager's job, does that sound sufficient? Obviously not.

Figure 1.1

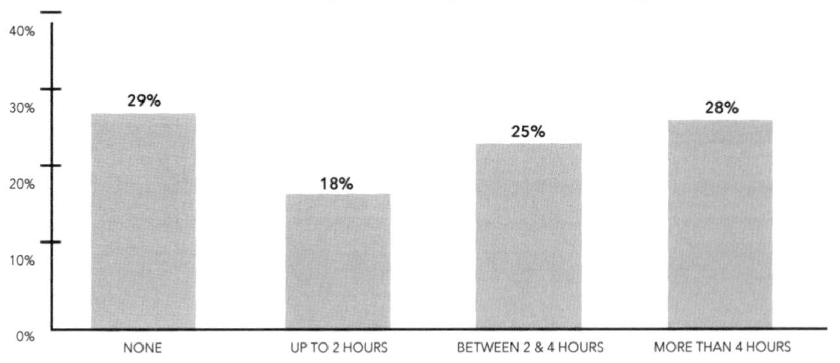

There are two more problems. The first is that a lot of this "training" is not particularly good. Have you ever been stuck in some horrible classroom or virtual management training session led by an instructor with seemingly no experience managing others? Or, if they once did manage others, it appears to have been decades ago? This has happened to me more than once. It can be a nightmare of a corporate-mandated experience, one that makes no clear contribution to your career.

The other problem is with transfer of training—applying what you have learned in training when you are back on the job. In this book I explain clearly what employees want from you. I lay out what to do and what not to do, based on what employees have told me in their own words. And I will give you advice that can be immediately put into practice in your daily interactions.

3. Unknowingly, you overestimate your competence as a people manager.

Like most other organizational psychologists, I have long known that when asked to rate themselves, most—though not all—managers tend to overestimate their competence.

Let me share a case in point. I asked a representative sample of 10,000 employees to evaluate the overall effectiveness of their managers. I also asked 1,000 managers to evaluate their own effectiveness using the same measures. Table 1.2 provides a comparison of the ratings.

Table 1.2

Overall Managerial Effectiveness: Employee Ratings vs. Manager Self-Ratings

Elements of Overall Managerial Effectiveness	Employee Rating Average Score*	Manager Self-Rating Average Score*	Difference	Difference Statistically Significant?
Work Management	3.70	4.33	-0.63	Yes
People Management	3.67	4.30	-0.63	Yes
Overall Effectiveness	3.91	4.33	-0.42	Yes
Outstanding Leader	3.63	4.10	-0.54	Yes
Overall Average	**3.73**	**4.27**	**-0.56**	**Yes**

*Rating scale: 1 = lowest and 5 = highest score.

The ratings managers give themselves are consistently higher on all four elements of overall effectiveness, and the overall average score of managerial self-ratings exceeds the ratings provided by employees by more than a half-point. That is a big perception-performance gap.

While this storyline is not new, it does reinforce the point. Employees are the most well-informed observers of managers' performance. Managers need the full commitment of employees to achieve higher levels of individual performance, better internal team relations, and higher team productivity. Employees are indicating that managers are not quite as good at people management as they think they are. There is room to grow, and this book gives you the advice you need to hear.

4. You want to create a superior work experience for your employees.

The popular term used to describe this is employee experience or "EX." Organizations have become increasingly concerned about creating an EX that will enable them to attract the talent they need, fully engage them, retain them, and even use them to advocate for the employer in recruiting more top talent to fuel the organization's growth and success.

It's only reasonable to assume that a manager influences the quality of EX for each and every employee. Question: *By how much*? Answer: *A bunch*.

I have EX scores for thousands of employees around the world. When I compare EX scores for employees working for managers separated by capability into the top, middle, and bottom employee-centric manager (ECM) categories, this is what I find:

- EX scores for those working for top-rated ECMs = 95%
- EX scores for those working for middle-rated ECMs = 70%
- EX scores for those working for bottom-rated ECMs = 21%

EX scores range from 0% to 100%. Nobody can score higher than 100%, and the top-rated ECMs are basically already there. Isn't that the kind of manager you want to be? This book helps you get there.

5. You want to create more engaged teams.

We just demonstrated that the ECM has an enormous impact on EX, and EX specialists tell us that EX is the means to employee engagement. In the past 20 years, we have heard a lot about employee engagement. Our science has evolved to the point that we know not only that employee engagement *correlates with* organizational performance, but that employee engagement is in fact a major *cause* of organizational performance.

Engaged employees are highly motivated, focused on important goals, and willing to apply discretionary effort. They are the people willing to go the extra mile to get the job done and inspire others to do the same.

We have demonstrated that ECMs influence EX. If EX is the means to employee engagement, it is only logical that ECMs also influence engagement. Let's compare engagement scores for three groups:

- Engagement scores for employees working for top-rated ECMs = 97%
- Engagement scores for employees working for middle-rated ECMs = 76%
- Engagement scores for employees working for bottom-rated ECMs = 20%

If it feels like you have already seen these results, that's because you have. The effect of being an ECM is fundamentally the same on engagement as it is on EX. Because EX is a means to employee engagement, this is not surprising. Being an ECM means you have employees who are highly motivated, focused on important goals, and willing to apply discretionary effort. Isn't that what you want to be? Read on.

6. You're looking for ways to enable a more positive and inclusive work environment.

Work is increasingly done by teams, not just an independent collection of employees who report to the same manager. As a manager, you want to get along well with all the people on your team, just as you want your team members to work well with one another. This is called *positive team chemistry*—when people genuinely feel respected as part of the team and cooperate well, and when conflicts are quickly and effectively resolved.

Overseeing a dysfunctional team is like playing a lead role in a horror movie, except the story is reality. Necessary communication is replaced with sarcasm and backbiting, problems fester, performance suffers, and people—including the most talented—are looking for the exit. This gets you recognized for all the *wrong* reasons.

Let's consider what team chemistry looks like under our three different scenarios:

- Team chemistry scores for employees working for top-rated ECMs = 99%
- Team chemistry scores for employees working for middle-rated ECMs = 75%
- Team chemistry scores for employees working for bottom-rated ECMs = 41%

Do you want great team chemistry? Look in the mirror. On a

five-point scale, how do you rate yourself as an ECM? Remember that, on average, employees rate managers about a half-point lower than they rate themselves. Read this book, put its advice into practice, gain that half-point or more, and become (or stay) a top-rated ECM.

7. Achieving higher levels of team performance is a top priority for you.

This is what it is all about. EX, employee engagement, and team chemistry are important contributors to your success as a manager, but how your team actually performs is what makes the biggest impression on your bosses and therefore most influences your career trajectory.

Of course, different teams produce different kinds of outputs, products, or services. But whether you are managing a fast food restaurant or a research and development lab for a medical device company, there are some common ways to evaluate your team's performance. Under your leadership, is your team highly productive in relation to the resources available to them, and are their products or services of high quality? Does your team consistently meet its goals on time? In essence, how effective is the team you lead?

Consider the outcomes below for managers slotted into three different levels of ECM capability:

- Team performance scores for teams working for top-rated ECMs = 99%
- Team performance scores for teams working for middle-rated ECMs = 75%

- Team performance scores for teams working for bottom-rated ECMs = 39%

To what level of team performance do you aspire? Some may be satisfied with middling performance; they may not be willing to invest in acquiring the knowledge and skills and adopting the values needed to genuinely excel. This book is not written for them. It is written for the manager who wants to excel at the highest level. If you are that manager, keep reading.

8. You'd love to boost your overall managerial effectiveness ratings.

Your own experience tells you that the higher your performance ratings, the greater your pay increases and the better your promotional opportunities. So, how do you improve your overall effectiveness ratings? The simple but proven answer: ***fully develop the eight employee-centric manager attributes.***

First, a little background: Many organizations around the world today use upward (180-degree) performance feedback systems. This involves employees rating their manager's performance. Researchers tell us that employees' views of their managers' performance is the most valid view. Why? Because employees are the best informed about how a manager operates. That only makes sense. Research also shows that employees' ratings of a manager's performance align with the ratings provided by that manager's own manager. This is reassuring.

So, how do I know that fully developing the eight ECM attributes is a sure pathway to greater overall effectiveness? I collected 180-degree performance ratings on over 10,000 managers and found that 67%

of their perceived overall effectiveness is explained by how they are rated on the ECM attributes. **This means that how employees rate managers on the ECM attributes determines two-thirds of their overall effectiveness rating** (see Figure 1.2). If you rate highly on these eight ECM attributes, you rate highly on overall performance. The reverse is also true: If you are rate poorly on the eight ECM attributes, you rate poorly on overall performance.

Figure 1.2

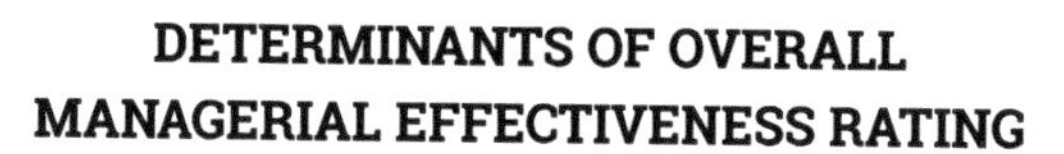

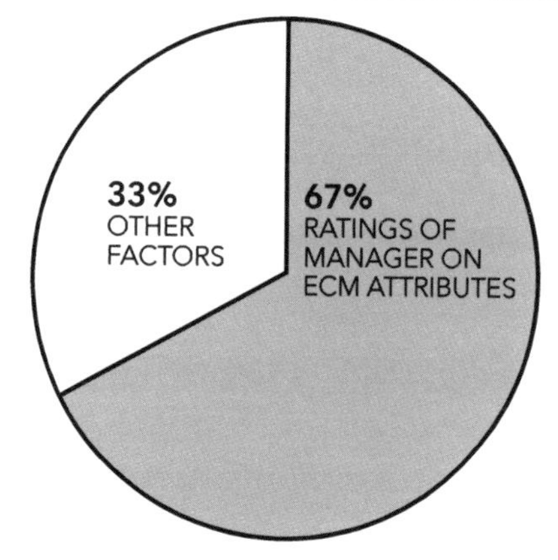

In this book, I share what you need to do to achieve the best performance reviews so that you can get what naturally follows—greater pay increases and better promotional opportunities.

9. You want an evidence-based pathway for employee, team, and personal success.

Let's make this easy. Figure 1.3 lays out your pathway to enhanced success. Everything I have shared with you in this chapter is based on research that is summarized in Figure 1.3.

Figure 1.3

5-1-2 Theory of Managerial Effectiveness

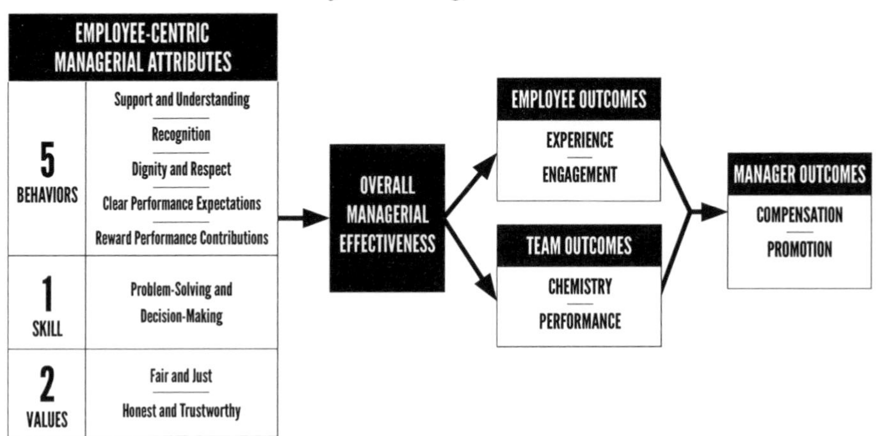

The 5-1-2 theory of managerial effectiveness states:

There are eight universal attributes employees prefer in their managers. Behavior-wise, employees want managers who (1) show support and understanding, (2) provide recognition, (3) treat employees with dignity and respect, (4) communicate clear performance expectations, and (5) reward performance contributions. Skill-wise, employees want managers who are competent in problem-solving and decision-making. Values-wise, employees want their managers to be (1) fair and just and (2) honest and trustworthy. Managers who demonstrate these attributes are seen by their employees as highly effective managers. Highly effective managers—those who demonstrate these attributes—contribute to a better experience for employees and higher levels of employee engagement. Teams overseen by these managers enjoy better team chemistry and higher overall performance. As a result, these managers gain higher compensation and greater promotional opportunities.

Does this describe you? More importantly, is this how your employees describe you? My research illuminates the pathway to feeling terrific about your job, fulfilling your potential as a manager, and positioning yourself—assuming you so desire—for bigger roles and higher pay.

I have given you nine reasons for reading this book, digesting its content, and applying its lessons. No one can do this for you; you must do it for yourself. If you are ready, let's roll.

CHAPTER 2

Eight Keys to Managerial Success:

Five Key Behaviors, One Key Skill, and Two Key Values

Most people managers I know approach their work with six (more or less) goals in mind:

1. **They want to get along well with the members of their team**. And who doesn't? After all, it's not much fun to deal with upsets in your key working relationships, especially when they happen time and time again.

2. **They want their team members to get along well with one another.** Regularly needing to resolve interpersonal conflict within a team is a drag on time and energy and makes everybody grumpy. Worse, it is a killer for team productivity.

3. **They want their teams to be highly engaged in their work.** Engaged employees are employees who are well suited for their work and mission oriented. They are confident of success and, most importantly, willing to go the extra mile to get the job done.

4. **They want their teams to operate at high levels of performance.** When all is said and done, this is fundamentally what your job is—to maximize the resources, human and otherwise—that have been entrusted to you. When you do it well, it's what gets you noticed in the *right* way by your own bosses.

5. **They want highly favorable performance reviews.** Being seen as competent is one of the three most important psychological needs we human beings have, and this is especially true for managers who want to grow in their careers (see the next goal).

6. **They want to maximize their rewards.** As with rank-and-file employees, rewards for managers typically fall into two categories: higher incomes and better opportunities for career growth. And how managers are seen by their bosses is typically the decisive factor in achieving this goal.

Are these your goals? Think about it. What in the above list is not an important goal to you? What goal personal to you is missing? You might express your goals in a slightly different way, but if you are like most people managers, your personal goals are all somehow included in this list.

So, how do you get there? What is the formula for how you "show up" to your employees in a way that advances you along the path of obtaining these goals, of achieving the success you want?

The Five Key Behaviors for Achieving Success as a People Manager

Employees at all levels in organizations, from frontline workers to those occupying executive suites, told me that they want their bosses to **do** five things. Remember, in this context we define behavior as actions you use to adjust to or influence behavior by your employees. Here are the five behaviors that employees want to see in their bosses:

1. Show Support and Understanding

This is the Big Daddy, or Big Momma, if you prefer, of what employees most want from their immediate bosses. Twenty-six percent of all employees worldwide identified this as the managerial attribute most important to them. Don't be fooled into thinking that this pertains only to frontline workers. In a follow-up study of employees based in the United States, executives (28%) were more likely to indicate this as their most important desire than mid-level managers (22%), frontline supervisors (20%), or employees classified as individual contributors (25%).

This attribute is so important that it naturally breaks down into two subcategories. *Support* refers to being present and accessible, providing help in daily activities, being encouraging, standing up for employees, and following through on employee concerns and issues. *Understanding* refers first and foremost to listening but also means being considerate and friendly, paying attention to employees' needs and difficulties, showing empathy, and developing healthy overall relationships with employees.

Is this how you show up to your employees?

2. Provide Recognition

One of the most interesting things about recognition is that it costs you nothing. All it takes is for you to be aware of its importance to employees and to take the time and exert the effort to make it happen. What I am talking about is psychological recognition or appreciation shown to employees for a job well done; this is the proverbial "pat on the back."

Recognition (13%) is the second most frequently identified desire that employees have of their bosses. At the same time, it is employee desire that managers most underappreciate in terms of positive impact on performance and commitment. If you as a people manager are failing to adequately recognize your employees, you are suboptimizing big time because recognition is one of the most important drivers of employee engagement, and we know that an engaged workforce is a more productive and successful workforce.

Recognition refers to complimenting and praising good work, giving employees credit for good ideas, and acknowledging employees for their loyalty to the job and the organization. It is important for people managers to recognize both teams and individuals. Managers who are good at this personalize recognition to the specifics of what an employee does well, and recognize the passion, skills, and abilities of employees, along with their concrete achievements.

Is this how you show up to your employees?

3. Treat Employees with Dignity and Respect

This isn't hard to understand because being treated with dignity and respect is something we all seek in all parts of our lives. In the work setting, being treated with dignity and respect is empowering; it gives us a sense of feeling validated to express our opinions and to act independently. It also shows that others care about us and want us to be treated in the same way they wish to be treated. Worldwide, almost one in ten (9%) employees indicated that this was the most important thing they wanted from their immediate manager.

In practice, treating employees with dignity and respect refers to the general notion of treating people well, as competent adults who want to make useful contributions to the team's efforts. It also involves trusting the experience employees bring to the job and showing respect for diverse working styles. It can also be demonstrated in the concern managers show for the welfare of their employees, such as the care managers take to ensure the safety and physical well-being of employees.

Is this how you show up to your employees?

4. Communicate Clear Performance Expectations

The theory of self-determination states that one of our three most basic psychological needs is to experience competence. In the work context, this means that we are motivated to do what is necessary to demonstrate mastery over our assigned work. Typically, though, we need to understand what mastery means, and we need feedback on how well we are doing our jobs so that our future efforts are even more successful. Worldwide, approximately one in eight employees (12%) identify communicating clear performance expectations as the most important thing they want from their immediate managers.

This is what managers do to fulfill this employee desire: They communicate work priorities, provide clear directions for the work assigned, and deliver honest and helpful feedback on how employees are performing. They also connect the work to the bigger purpose of the organization, that is, to its mission and its values. The way a manager communicates is also crucial. What employees want is timely communication that is clear, concise, honest, and transparent. As a result, employees will understand what is expected in terms of productivity, quality, and timeliness.

Is this how you show up to your employees?

5. Reward Performance Contributions

This is the quid pro quo of the work exchange. Employees bring their knowledge, skills, abilities, and personality characteristics to the job, perform their work, and expect to be rewarded fairly for their contributions. But the rewards employees are looking for are not limited to just a paycheck. They also want to be rewarded with more and better job and career opportunities.

Interestingly, of the eight attributes employees most want in a manager, this is the one that ties for last place in terms of how frequently it was voiced. Only 8% of the world's workforce said that this is what they most want from their manager. That may be because it is a presumed "given"; perhaps even more likely, the low percentage might be explained by a belief that reward policy falls under the responsibility of the organization as a whole, where pay-raise targets and training budgets are established. Still, it is a key consideration for all employees, regardless of gender, age, or educational level.

When employees state that what they most want from their manager is to be rewarded for their performance contributions, they mean one of two things. Most obviously, they mean they want managers who advocate for fair and higher compensation for them. They want managers who invest the time and energy to find out what rewards are most relevant to them. They want managers who can clearly communicate what it takes to earn a raise and—when bonuses or incentives are involved—to ensure that performance goals are realistic and achievable.

But more training and development for personal growth is also a form of rewarding the performance contributions of employees. Employees want their managers to provide opportunities for relevant skills training and to articulate a clear career path for them. They want more than simply a picture of realistic future possibilities; they also want their managers to ensure they have real opportunities for development, promotions, and career growth. This might involve removing roadblocks to development opportunities and helping employees build the skills needed for future roles in the organization.

Is this how you show up to your employees?

The One Key Skill for Achieving Success as a People Manager

Think of a skill as a behavior you demonstrate well because you have practiced and practiced and practiced it. Growing up, I was not very skilled at piano playing because I did not like to practice. I would rather be out playing basketball or baseball with the other kids in the neighborhood. My parents finally realized that my piano lessons were a poor investment: Even my piano teacher told them it was a waste of money! I was not getting any better at playing the piano because I did not practice.

A skill is something you are good at because it is something you have practiced. As a result of your practice, you develop an expertise.

1. Demonstrate Competence in Problem-Solving and Decision-Making

Employees want to work for managers who are experts in problem-solving and decision-making. It is not that employees simply want managers to solve problems and make decisions. Rather, they want their managers to be good at it—to be skilled at it. The reasons are obvious. When you are good at problem-solving and decision-making, your employees are better able to get their work done and done well. And when your employees are better able to get their jobs done, their basic need to feel competent in their work is satisfied. Their frustration with work obstacles fades away while their self-esteem improves. They are happier in their jobs and more engaged in their work because the path to their goal has been cleared.

Now, to be sure, employees are expected to solve some problems and make some decisions on their own. In fact, most employees want this sense of autonomy in how they go about their work. That is not in dispute. As workers climb the organizational ladder, they are increasingly expected to solve more difficult problems and make more challenging decisions.

But at every level in the organization, except for the very top position, managers are also subordinates. While they are expected to nurture their skills in problem-solving and decision-making, there are still occasions where they need help from their bosses.

In addition, there are obviously times when a problem arises, or a decision must be made in which an employee simply lacks the authority to move forward.

Employees want managers who can make good decisions quickly. They want to work for managers who can solve problems with appropriate, workable solutions. They want their managers to remove roadblocks that get in the way of getting the work done. In effect, employees want managers who understand the responsibility they have to their employees and are competent in clearing the path to their job success. Employees do want the autonomy to do their own jobs and do them competently. But when they need help, they want to be able to turn to a manager who can provide that help, one with good overall supervision, management, and leadership skills.

Is this how you show up to your employees?

The Two Key Values for Achieving Success as a People Manager

By definition, personal values are important to you. Values represent the principles or standards by which behavior is judged. In most academic studies of leadership, the personal values of leaders are barely discussed, but when employees were asked to identify what they most want from their immediate managers, they clearly identified two critical values. In fact, almost one in five employees identified a value—a standard of behavior—as what they most wanted from their bosses.

1. Fair and Just

Have you ever been treated unfairly at work? If so, you know what this means. A common cause of perceived unfairness is managers making employee-related decisions that produce unequal treatment of employees. For example, Joe is late for work and is sent home for the day. Sally is late for work and is encouraged to try a little harder and to make up the lost time over her lunch hour. Same infraction, different outcome.

Another likely cause of perceived unfairness is that managers follow different processes in making employee-related decisions. The manager notices that Joe is late and sends Joe home, no questions asked. Sally is also late but in a conversation with Sally, the manager learns that her dog was sick and that she had to arrange for its care. Same infraction, different process.

Yet another cause of perceived unfairness has to do with setting different expectations for employees. When Sally was hired, she was told that every late arrival at work would lead to a disciplinary action. When Joe was hired, no such information was shared with him. Same infraction, different levels of shared information.

These are simple examples used to illustrate a crucial point; you can no doubt think of examples from your own experience to make the same points. The truth is that much of what we know about fair and just treatment of employees is a result of their violations; that is, through studying examples of unjust or unfair treatment. Unfairness and injustice are bad business, and employees sniff it out right away. This kind of treatment of employees leads to a host of unwanted outcomes: lower job satisfaction, lower employee engagement, lower levels of commitment to the team and the organization as a whole, lower interest in being a good organizational citizen, and unwanted voluntary resignations. After all, why should employees give their best and go out of their way to help an unfair or unjust manager succeed?

So, when employees say that want a manager who is fair and just, they mean they want a manager who provides equal and fair treatment of all employees, a manager who acts with objectivity and consistency. And they want a manager who judges employees on the basis of their work performance, not on their individual characteristics like gender, race, or ethnic origin.

Is this how you show up to your employees?

2. Honest and Trustworthy

As with being fair and just, being honest and trustworthy represents a value that employees prize in their managers. Put yourself in the position of being deceived by your manager or hearing them say one thing but do another, perhaps even the opposite of what they preach. How does that make you feel? If your manager is not honest and trustworthy, what can you do? Who can you turn to? It can be a lonely and miserable place, and employees simply hate it. Unfortunately, most of us have had such experiences.

We all know what being honest means. It means you tell the truth and lay out the facts as they are. It means you are sincere, frank, candid, and forthright. It means you are free of deceit, neither concealing nor misrepresenting the truth. The bosom buddy of being honest is being trustworthy. Where you find one value, you will undoubtedly find the other. Being trustworthy means that people can rely on you. It means they can depend on you to be honest and truthful. It is hard to put a price on the importance of this to your employees, and we know what happens when it is absent. It leads to cynicism and distrust, and your employees will soon learn to become skeptical of what you say. They will be trying to figure out your angle, to guess what's in the "deal" for you. Why? Because they no longer trust you and have come to see you as being motivated fundamentally by self-interest, not the interest of the team or the greater organization.

But when employees see you as living the values of honesty and trustworthiness, it tends to cover up other shortcomings. Employees are more loyal to you and the team. They are willing to go the extra mile to get the job done. They are willing to do the inconvenient but necessary things to meet a deadline or satisfy a customer. Being honest and trustworthy is not a skill, and it is not expertise; it is a value-based choice that reflects your personal standard of behavior.

When employees say they want a manager who is honest and trustworthy, they are describing a manager who is forthright and transparent. They are describing a manager who is sincere, truthful, and reliable. This is a manager who acts with integrity, who not only is honest but also acts from a set of strong moral principles and displays a strong sense of moral uprightness in their actions.

Is this how you show up to your employees?

In the chapters that follow, I have more to say about each of these attributes. I outline dos and don'ts and give you solid recommendations for how to grow and develop in each one of these attributes. I share actual incidents from the employee perspective that portray the good and the bad of how managers reveal their true colors. Remember this reality: The manager who displays these ECM attributes is one who gets along well with their employees and leads a team with positive interpersonal chemistry and a record of top performance. Such a manager is the one who receives highly favorable performance reviews and is in line for higher pay and better job opportunities. Does that sound appealing? Keep reading, and I will share with you how to achieve these and other great outcomes.

CHAPTER 3

Practicing the Five Key Behaviors Employees Value Most

You know by now that five of the managerial attributes employees most want and value from you are behaviors. As a manager you use behaviors to adjust to or influence your employees. That raises a lot of questions: most generally, how does this work on the job? How do I use these behaviors to influence employees to become more motivated in their work, to make a greater commitment to my team and the larger organization, and to perform at higher levels?

To help you answer these questions, I provide a variety of different insights and recommendations in this chapter. First, I quickly review how employees define each behavior. I then outline how each behavior can be used to motivate employees and how each behavior can be used to frustrate employees. Next, I share advice on how you can put these behaviors into practice to achieve your goals as a manager. This is followed by a profile of a manager who excels at demonstrating each behavior, and quotations from employees on their positive and negative experiences with managers. Finally, I share key takeaways you can incorporate into your daily routine. We go through one behavior at a time.

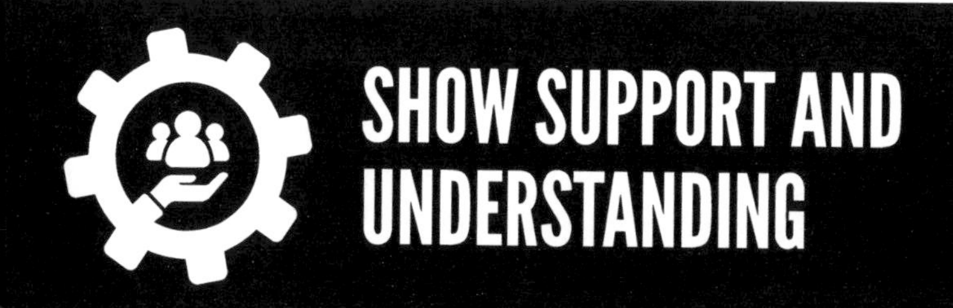

SHOW SUPPORT AND UNDERSTANDING

As we saw in chapter 2, this attribute is so important that it naturally breaks down into two subcategories. *Support* refers to being present and accessible, providing help in daily activities, being encouraging, standing up for employees, and following through on employee concerns and issues. *Understanding* refers first and foremost to listening but also to being considerate and friendly, paying attention to employees' needs and difficulties, showing empathy, and developing healthy overall relationships with employees.

Employees provided a lot of input on the topic of support and understanding, especially in terms of what to do to display this attribute. This is what employees specifically want from you:

- Get to know each employee sufficiently well that you understand their current capabilities, training and development needs, and goals.

- When listening to employees describe their concerns, respond in a way that shows that you are genuine and supportive; in other words, be empathetic.

- Make employee job satisfaction a priority. Understand that employee job satisfaction is determined by comparing what employees want from their job and what they see as their current reality.

- Ensure employees know who you are; that is, your priorities, your values, and some things about your history and you as a person.
- When necessary, *stick up for your employees.* Show them that you have their back and show them that you believe in them.

What not to do in showing support and understanding:

- Don't be absent or inaccessible. It does not really matter how busy you think you are; it is hard for a manager to be helpful if they are never around or can't be found.
- Don't fail to follow through on employee concerns. It often takes courage for employees to share their work-related concerns openly and honestly with you. You will not build employee commitment by failing to follow up on these concerns.
- Don't show a lack of regard for employee well-being in terms of safety, workload, and important matters in their personal lives that affect their work.
- Don't demonstrate impatience, offer immediate criticism, or adopt a judgmental attitude when employees come to you with a problem that needs to be solved.
- Don't be afraid to have a little fun in the workplace. Employees want to work with managers who are real people. Never showing your fun side to employees is a missed opportunity to build the connections that are important to employee commitment.

My advice for showing support and understanding

Think of this list as the most important recommendations for how to show support for and consideration to your employees. They do not constitute everything you can do to be understanding and supportive; they are the ones that bubbled up to the top of the list after I surveyed tens of thousands of employees worldwide:

- Show genuine interest in your employees. Effective people managers take a sincere interest in their employees' well-being and their lives outside of work. Listening to employees and remembering prior conversations you have had with them reassures employees that you are truly listening and that you truly care.
- Be an effective listener. While contributing to a conversation is important, taking time to listen to and understand others is critical to being—and being seen—as a supportive manager. When you listen effectively to your employees, more innovative solutions, more buy-in to the future, and more respect for you will follow.
- Conduct one-on-one meetings with employees on a consistent basis. Regularly meeting this way with employees is a vital step in showing support and interest in their work. Ongoing meetings help build and deepen rapport, encourage both parties to raise issues proactively, and provide an opportunity for informal feedback. Some settings—such as manufacturing or process work settings—may make this nearly impossible. But the manager who can pull this off in one way or another will gain a lot.

- Provide proper tools, technology, and materials. After all, how can your employees be expected to do their jobs effectively if you don't provide them with the tools, technology, equipment, and support they need? Isn't this the most basic definition of being supportive?
- Address low morale. When employees seem to be having difficulty or are experiencing low morale, talk to them to find out what is causing the problem. Identify what you can do to make things better, and then follow up! That is your job and that is how you can really "show" support and understanding.

MANAGER PROFILE

Nomare Sattar

Nomare Sattar manages a team of 18 consultants at The Shelby Group, a firm specializing in procurement transformation for large organizations. Since Nomare joined the firm eight years ago, Shelby has grown an average of 25% annually, working with global brands to implement procurement infrastructure in over 90 countries.

To keep up with its rapid growth rate, Shelby has created a sophisticated process for selecting, training, and developing consulting talent and managers. Every employee is assigned a mentor, an HR manager, and a direct supervisor, and performance is evaluated three times annually against precisely defined personal development milestones. Nomare's exceptionally strong people-management skills have enabled him to rise quickly through the ranks to his current position as a senior manager, leading teams assigned to multimillion-dollar projects around the world.

Q What's unique about the way that Shelby develops managers and consultants?

Many in our industry hire consultants based on experience, but the procurement transformation field is new, and experienced consultants are in short supply. Shelby hires based on attitude, intellect, and ability—not specific experience within the field. This enables us to develop the specific hard and soft skills that define our competitive advantage. Since beginning as an entry-level consultant eight years ago, I have benefitted from and helped shape this program.

Q How has demonstrating support and understanding for employees influenced your career and the careers of team members under your supervision?

A year ago, my answer would have been fundamentally different. Before the 2020-2021 pandemic, I took a very hands-on approach to helping team members develop their skills during on-site deployments, where each person is assigned to a different workstream. Rather than waiting for assignments to be completed, I bounced between team members as the work progressed. I helped troubleshoot issues and asked each person to review how they had arrived at a given conclusion. I believe in a learning-by-doing approach to skills development, but these interactions weren't just about the work. We also discussed non-project-related challenges, like difficulty dealing with another team member or nervousness about being asked to present to the client. By asking questions, I was often able to help employees diagnose and address the root causes of the issue.

Today, face-to-face interactions are no longer possible. The pandemic has changed our whole way of working together. Many of the fun parts of the job have disappeared. Traveling to interesting cities around the globe, team outings to sample local cuisine or sightsee—the very things that made consulting cool—came to an abrupt end as everything went virtual overnight.

Q How did you adjust your style of management and what impact has the pandemic had on your team members?

Initially, everyone's attitude was great. Our culture is very much like a family, and there was a shared sense that we could get through this together. As the weeks wore on, Zoom fatigue took its toll. I began to see some inconsistencies and decreased morale. I knew we needed to rethink how we supported employees. We were still able to do learning by doing virtually, but this didn't address the emotional consequences of such a significant change in the work environment. So, we made adjustments. We shifted from weekly one-on-one interactions to check-ins at the start and end of each workday. These informal phone chats sometime last only a few minutes, but an experienced mentor can detect when employees are dealing with a problem, such as accommodating their children's schedules or other personal responsibilities, and offer guidance or simply a sympathetic ear. We also started virtual team happy hours and livened up team meetings with fun and sometimes goofy activities. These new approaches have had a positive impact. But we're not through tweaking: It may sound clichéd, but continuous improvement is definitely baked into our corporate culture.

Q Can you think of an example when demonstrating support and understanding made a significant difference in the career of a specific employee?

Among the many examples, one in particular comes to mind. For individuals who excel, opportunities for promotion and economic rewards at Shelby can come at a steady pace. A few years ago, one of my direct reports, Ahmed, was up for a promotion to become a senior consultant. He had the smarts and the skills, but everyone on the promotion review team felt something was missing. I had a hunch about what the problem might be, and I scheduled a touch-base conversation. After a series of routine questions about how things were going and how he was feeling about the job, I asked him to think about where he wanted to be in five years and to describe the ideal job. He said he'd like to work as a management consultant. I asked him to tell me what skills he thought he'd need to be successful in that role. As he listed the skills, a smile came over his face. He realized something that I had already known. Outside of technical knowledge unique to procurement, the skills and abilities that Shelby consultants learn are identical to those used by management consultants. I helped him understand that his ability to improve and apply these skills while working with clients at Shelby was far greater than if he were to take an entry-level position at a big-name management consulting firm. After this session, Ahmed's attitude changed significantly—not just toward the job but in his interactions with team members. He's now one of our highest-rated managers. Last year, he earned three consecutive performance recognitions. Ahmed has made a lot of progress; he definitely excels at demonstrating support and understanding to the employees he manages.

Q What advice do you have for other managers regarding showing support and understanding to employees?

We're all stressed and overworked. As a manager, your greatest responsibility is helping employees succeed. No matter how busy you are, take the time to see the world through each employee's eyes. Let them know you care about them as individuals. Rather than simply telling them what to do, ask them questions that will help them take ownership of solutions.

"My manager is understanding of the difficulties that I am facing with the school year. I have more students than ever before, on top of teaching virtually and in person at the same time. My manager offered me the support needed to be able to teach effectively."

–PROFESSIONAL, EDUCATION, FEMALE, 23

Color commentary: Being a teacher presents a wide array of challenges, but those challenges can be especially difficult when unexpected external circumstances (like the 2020–2021 COVID-19 pandemic) kick in. This manager shows up as one who listens, who understands, and who is empathetic to the challenges facing their employees. And the manager responds with the type of support specifically aimed at meeting the need. The result? Teachers stay in the game and perform their jobs effectively.

"There was a breakdown in my delivery car, so my manager came to my rescue to satisfy the requirement to meet the customer delivery deadline."

–MANAGER, TRANSPORTATION, MALE, 30

Color commentary: Most employees want to meet the demands of their jobs. They genuinely want to perform up to the standards expected of them, but sometimes bad things happen that they cannot control. In this case, the manager jumped in with very personal involvement. Maybe there were other options for meeting the performance standard, and maybe there weren't. The point is that the manager did what was necessary to bail out the employee and keep the organization's standards and reputation intact. How do you suppose this episode impacted the loyalty of this employee toward that manager?

"I had and am still having a hard time with the deaths resulting from COVID. I cannot speak about it without crying. When COVID cases recently picked up again, I had a discussion with my manager about my everyday difficulties. She understood, and we agreed that I would not take COVID patients; if my ICU ends up being all COVID like it was in the spring, I will transfer to another unit."

–PROFESSIONAL, HEALTH CARE, FEMALE, 49

Color commentary: The pandemic has highlighted how health care workers are on the front line of combating what is all too often a mortal enemy. We have always known this to be true, but we have a much greater appreciation of it now than ever before. This employee is suffering from a high and unremitting level of workplace stress. The manager in question was likely stretched thin in terms of staffing options, but her response was first to acknowledge that the employee had reached their limit and second, to adopt solutions that kept the employee onboard and offered a sense of hope for the future.

"My manager meets with me one-on-one monthly to discuss how my job is going, what if anything I'm struggling with, and any ideas or suggestions I have to make my work more effective. This makes me feel that my opinions and suggestions matter."

–PROFESSIONAL, EDUCATION, FEMALE, 47

Color commentary: Monthly one-on-one meetings with employees is not a new concept; in fact, some managers consider them to be a nuisance or waste of time. But think about what this manager is communicating to this employee: "I want you to do well. I want to know what obstacles you are facing so that together we can overcome them and make sure your work flows smoothly." This is the essence of proactive listening, empowering the employee, and taking corrective joint action as needed. It is not surprising that this employee feels valued.

"My manager is always watching our backs with upper-level managers. This allows us to do our jobs with excellence. She gives us credit for our successes, puts us in for awards, and fights for our training, promotion, and pay."

–TECHNICIAN, GOVERNMENT, MALE, 59

Color commentary: Well, I don't know if the work performance of this employee and his coworkers is truly excellent, but I do know they have high regard for their manager. Why? Look at all the employee-centric attributes on display: support (and understanding), recognition, clear performance expectations, and reward performance contributions. Apparently, these employees are indeed high-performing or their manager would not be advocating that they be treated as such. Who wouldn't want to be on this team?

"I brought a problem to my manager's attention, and she let me explain what I think would work best moving forward. She understood that I am the one out there doing the job and I would have the best understanding of the solution. She got back to me quickly and trusted me to make the decision."

–CLERK, HEALTH CARE, FEMALE, 29

Color commentary: This is something employees really want: to work for a manager who values their opinion. This manager operates with the belief that frontline employees are well informed and can not only easily identify what is getting in the way of getting the job done but also suggest reasonable, workable solutions. This is called *participative management*. Notice that the manager also places a high value on her employee's time, as reflected in how quickly she gets back to the employee. This enables the employee to get on with the job. The result? A happy employee who feels valued and competent.

"During meetings, my manager is sometimes distracted IM'ing others regarding work issues when it should be our one-on-one time. This makes me feel unimportant and makes me less likely to open up."

–PROFESSIONAL, BANKING, FEMALE, 41

Color commentary: If your goal is to send a message to your subordinates that you are not a good listener, then do not make eye contact in your meetings with them; instead, make sure you are multitasking. When a manager behaves this way, what conclusion is the employee expected to draw? Sure, you may be a busy manager with too much crammed into your own work schedule, but the impact of behaving this way is summarized by the quote above, which implies this: *as a manager you don't treat my interactions with you as important; as a result, I am not going to open up with you about what is happening in my job, be it good or bad.* The employee feels discounted, and the manager may lose out on some important information that could impact individual or team engagement and performance.

"I remember working a late shift where I was closing the bakery, and I was also on my menstrual cycle. My emotions were running high, and that day was the worst time to be working with my manager because he showed little or no patience when it came to answering some of my questions. It made me feel like I couldn't even come to him for help because of his impatience. In other words, I felt terrible."

–PROFESSIONAL, RETAIL, FEMALE, 29

Color commentary: Okay, for many people, this quote may include too much information. At the same time, it is open and forthcoming and does portray a very genuine incident. This manager was apparently oblivious to how his employee was feeling on this particular day. On top of that, the manager has a reputation, deserved or not, for being impatient with questions and requests from employees. It doesn't sound like this manager is very approachable at any time or that he shows an acceptable level of emotional intelligence. At least, that is the message he is sending his employees. This is the polar opposite of being supportive and understanding.

"My manager forces us to use things that actually make the job more difficult and add no benefit. When we suggest other options for getting the work done, he doesn't listen and yells at us if we try to change things."

–LABORER, MALE, 23

Color commentary: We have already noted most employees want to do a good job and be seen as competent at their work. They also expect their managers to remove obstacles to getting work done efficiently. In this incident, we of course can't know which work processes are most efficient, but it is apparent that employees feel stifled in their efforts to make it easier for them to do their work. It is not merely that they don't feel heard; they feel punished for offering suggestions for improvement. Even if their proposals are ultimately deemed unworkable, shouldn't a manager explain why? This manager seems content to allow employees to remain in the dark, be frustrated, and feel punished for wanting things to be better. How much energy is being wasted by this approach to managing others?

"I don't feel supported by my manager for not letting me use vacation time and always guilting me into working extra hours even when I do not receive any overtime pay or comp time."

–PROFESSIONAL, HEALTH CARE, FEMALE, 33

Color commentary: This is a manager who takes advantage of employees—simply put, it is a form of abuse. Vacation time is typically part of a total pay and benefits package, and this manager appears to be denying the employee what is rightfully hers. It would appear this manager is invested only in meeting their own goals, regardless of who must pay the price. Taking advantage of others is no way to show support and understanding. As is often the case, managers deficient in this attribute are also likely to be unfair and unjust.

"Honestly, my managers pretend to understand us but they just say things so you'll leave them alone. We are stressed out and scared, and nobody is being hired to help with the workload."

–SUPERVISOR, RETAIL, FEMALE, 29

Color commentary: This is called *clueless management*. There are all kinds of failures here. First, the managers don't seem to know or understand what is causing employees to be stressed out. Work stress is simple to understand—it occurs when the demands of work outstrip the resources available to employees. Second, the useless responses that managers provide are just that: they do nothing to address the problem. Eventually, employees come to understand that interactions with these managers are a waste of time. Third, these managers are shirking their responsibilities when it comes to managing team performance. Where is the plan for decreasing stress by aligning resources to match the increased demand? Not only are these managers "losers" when it comes to problem-solving, they are being fundamentally unfair to their employees. They don't deserve the compensation that comes with the manager job title.

"During the interview process, my manager made me feel as if the position I was applying for was important. I felt happy and relieved that I had found a decent position. The job turned out not to be what I was told. The long-term consequences are a false sense of trust and deceit. Now, I can't trust his decisions or his intentions."

–LABORER, AGRICULTURE, MALE, 30

Color commentary: It is easy to understand why this employee feels he works for a manager who doesn't support and understand him. Trust was broken when the manager oversold the job and that "promise" clashed with the reality. Let's face it; it is hard, in fact almost impossible, for a manager to overcome the opinion that they are willing to shade the truth (or outright lie) to achieve personal gain. These are never the managers who build loyal and committed teams. Maybe in this case there was an "honest" misunderstanding of what the job was all about. Who knows? But given the ongoing lack of trust this employee has in this manager, it doesn't seem the manager deserves the benefit of the doubt. He certainly hasn't done enough to change the initial impression.

Key Takeaways

1. Listen empathetically to the work challenges your employees are facing.
2. Invest time and energy in finding and implementing solutions to work-related problems; in a crisis, you may have to step in and do the work.
3. Watch the stress levels of your employees closely and adjust work assignments as needed.
4. Value the opinions of your frontline workers because they are often the best informed.
5. Make sure your employees are given credit for their successes and that higher levels of management are aware of their good work.
6. Treat your interactions with your employees as important; don't discount them by being distracted or multitasking.
7. Respond with patience to questions and requests; give employees, especially newer or less experienced employees, the guidance they need.
8. Take advantage of employee ideas and suggestions for how to improve workflow.
9. Make sure employees are treated fairly; never take advantage of them.
10. Deliver on your promises; broken trust is hard to repair.

PROVIDE RECOGNITION

This costs so little and means so much. One of the startling facts I discovered along the way is how important recognition is to employees and how tone-deaf many managers are to that importance. In a recent survey of 15,000 workers in the United States, 13% indicated that recognition is the most important thing they want from their immediate manager. In a survey of 1,000 managers, how many indicated that recognition is the thing their employees most want from them? Answer: a measly 1%. That means only one in every hundred managers surveyed identified recognition as what employees most want—a clear mismatch with the employee perspective.

Let's start to change that by once again defining recognition based on the voices of employees. *Recognition* refers to complimenting and praising good work, giving employees credit for good ideas, and acknowledging employees for their loyalty to the job and the organization. Employees state that it is important for people managers to recognize both teams and individuals. According to employees, managers who are good at this personalize recognition to the specifics of what an employee does well; they recognize the passion, skills, and abilities of employees, along with their achievements.

So, here is what to do to provide recognition in a way that matters to employees. Again, this comes straight from employees' own voices:

- Offer a simple thank-you when employees are working hard and overcoming unusual obstacles to get the job done.
- Be timely with your recognition: Real-time recognition has the most genuine and long-lasting impact.
- Show appreciation for the level of expertise employees have developed in their time on the job and recognize the passion and energy they bring to their work.
- Tailor recognition to the individual employee; learn how each person likes to be recognized (e.g., publicly vs. privately) and personalize the recognition accordingly.
- Provide recognition face-to-face. Since that may not always be possible, especially with remote workers, adapt to find a way to make this happen if possible. Being remote does not mean that the importance of recognition disappears.

According to employees, this is what not to do in providing recognition:

- Don't take personal credit for good ideas employees have provided.
- Don't be inconsistent in your recognition practices by, for example, treating employees differently in handing out praise for good work.
- Don't recognize only the "team" for good work when in fact the team's good performance was solely or largely due to the special efforts of only one or two employees.
- Don't make providing recognition seem like a chore. Even the appearance of insincerity demolishes the purpose and upside of recognition.

- Don't add criticism or negative feedback along with the recognition. Going negative while complimenting good work is all that recognition recipients may remember.

My advice for providing recognition

We know a lot about recognition and its positive impact on the motivation and performance of employees; in fact, entire books have been devoted to this topic. In addition to what is listed above, here is my advice, condensed to the basic and most important items:

- **Recognize your employees' good work frequently.** Of course, you must be sincere when doing this, but providing recognition to employees is key to ensuring they feel valued and that their work is appreciated. Whether it is a handwritten note or a shout-out in a meeting, managers who provide frequent recognition to their employees have a powerful positive influence on their engagement and productivity.
- **Be specific about the aspect of the employee contribution you are recognizing.** Recognition will have a greater influence on future employee behavior when you are very clear about what you are recognizing. Your recognition will be much more powerful when it is tied to a specific goal, accomplishment, or behavior.
- **In your recognition of your employees' good work, make a connection to the bigger picture.** Employees want to feel part of the larger organization and know that what they are doing is having an impact. When you fail to provide recognition in a way that ties it to the organization's goals, you miss a chance to help employees see how they are contributing to the organization's overall mission.

- **Celebrate both small and big wins.** Big wins are often the result of a succession of small wins. Overlooking the small wins along the way is a missed opportunity to boost employee confidence and motivation. Sure, at the end of the day, the big wins are what grab headlines, but how much faster could you get there with a highly motivated and recognized team?
- **Recognize loyalty to the job and to the organization.** If you work for a larger enterprise, this is especially relevant because it is part of your responsibility as a manager to encourage loyalty to the organization. Some organizations think their best interests are served by creating a constant churn of employees. These are typically organizations that have achieved initial success but have not yet shown the ability to sustain that success over time. Talented, committed, and recognized employees are key to the longer-term success of an organization. It won't happen without them, and you can help with employee retention by recognizing the allegiance of employees and celebrating their work anniversaries.

MANAGER PROFILE
Sarah Downs

Sarah Downs is the Director of Health Programming and Delivery at WellSpark Health, a leading well-being, disease prevention, and management company. She manages a team of eight direct reports and is responsible for delivering its diabetes prevention and non-clinical health programs. WellSpark's programs motivate employees to make healthy lifestyle and behavior changes and help employers reduce future health care costs, improve workforce productivity and engagement, and reduce absenteeism. Based in Connecticut, WellSpark is part of the EmblemHealth family of companies, serving public and private sector employers throughout the United States.

Q How did your career as a manager get started?

I received a master's degree in public health from The Ohio State University, with a concentration in health behavior and health promotion. After graduation, I went to work for the American Cancer Society, where I recruited and managed volunteers to run the organization's programs throughout central Ohio. This early experience was crucial in my development as a manager. Motivating teams of people who aren't getting paid isn't easy. After some trial and error, I learned that when I recognized individuals for their strengths and unique contributions, they became more engaged and productive. For me, this was a Management 101 lesson that has stuck with me ever since.

Next, I worked as a health coach and team leader for one of the country's largest health insurance companies. During this time, I worked with a manager who passed off many of her responsibilities to me, only to take credit for my accomplishments. This, of course, did not engender positive feelings, and it ultimately led to my decision to leave the company. The lesson I learned, however, was important. When people don't feel good about the contributions they make, they go work elsewhere. One of my favorite quotes from Maya Angelou sums it up nicely: "I've learned that people will forget what you said, people will forget what you did, but people will never forget how you made them feel." My job as a manager is to put people in the right roles and provide them with the support and recognition they need to feel good about their contributions daily.

How do you practice recognition as a manager?

I believe that to be effective, recognition must be truthful, authentic, and specific. Telling someone they did a great job isn't enough. I always try to acknowledge a particular behavior or action someone took that made a difference. I try to stay in constant touch with my teams by monitoring our platforms for collaboration and recognition. And I do frequent check-ins to see how people are doing. In addition to initiating recognition, I also try to find ways to amplify praise from others. Recently, one of our team leaders was congratulated by a senior manager on a job well done. I weighed in by acknowledging the success while also recognizing the contributions of specific individuals without whom that success would not have been possible.

Q How has your training as a health coach made you a better manager?

It has been immensely valuable. The job of a health coach is to help others become their best selves. You do this by understanding the whole person and what makes people tick. A great health coach empowers people to take action through motivation, active listening, and guided discussion. By applying these skills and abilities in the workplace, people excel, develop a stronger sense of self-worth, and accomplish things they may never have thought possible.

Q Can you recall a time when recognizing someone impacted performance?

Several years ago, we were facing a tight deadline on a critical project. One of the team members, who is a true perfectionist, was causing a bottleneck. Others involved in the project were worried about having enough time to complete their tasks. While my initial inclination was to criticize her for holding things up, I decided instead to recognize this individual for the passion and attention to detail she put into her work. I then asked her to step back and see the larger picture, not just the portion of the project she owned. Through a series of discussions, which weren't always easy, we formed an alliance. I agreed to help make sure that she had the support tools and time she needed to do her work, and she committed to make meeting deadlines a top priority, even if it meant settling for less than her usual 110% effort. Last year, during her annual review, she said learning to recognize that her strengths could also be a liability had made a significant difference in both her professional and personal lives. Her progress has been tremendous, and the sky is the limit for her career advancement in our organization.

Q What advice do you have for managers who want to get better at recognizing employees?

First, I think it is essential to understand that recognition is one of your most important responsibilities as a manager. When you take a genuine interest in helping people advance their careers and recognize them for their contributions, large or small, they feel valued, which creates a vital emotional connection. It is imperative now that we're working remotely, and all are suffering from feelings of isolation. Next, I believe every manager should make recognition part of their daily routine. It's not something you can put off and do when you have spare time. It doesn't take much time to include recognition in group meetings, during one-on-one touch-base sessions, or in chance encounters. Finally, you should find a mentor you can trust to provide you with objective feedback on improving your interactions up and down the corporate ladder. I have been very fortunate in my career to have worked with mentors who helped me understand my strengths and weaknesses and inspired me to continue to learn, grow, and improve as a manager and as a person.

"I have never had a time when my manager has done a lousy job at recognizing me. She appropriately and consistently commends and recognizes exemplary service and a good work ethic."

–SUPERVISOR, TRANSPORTATION, FEMALE, 42

Color commentary: This manager gets an A+ for consistently recognizing behaviors that are so highly valued by employers. Managers want employees who provide outstanding service and put in an honest day's work. One of the best ways to keep that coming is to show appreciation to those who deliver. Thorndike's law of effect instructs us that behavior followed by a positive outcome is likely to repeated. Smart managers are the ones who use psychological appreciation to reinforce the behavior they want in their employees.

"I came in a week early while recuperating from major surgery to help get tax bills ready to go out for the tax office. My supervisor made a point to tell the higher-ups that even though I was hurting, I went above and beyond to get the job done."

–CLERK, GOVERNMENT, FEMALE, 51

Color commentary: Wow—an employee in a professional office setting who is willing to sacrifice physical comfort and disrupt the healing process to help her employer meet production goals is indeed going above and beyond the call of duty. The employee's effort certainly deserved to be recognized, and this supervisor did something that employees crave—being put in the spotlight in front of the chain of command. Not only is the employee recognized in the here and now, but future promotional opportunities have also just increased.

"My manager hired me at the seasonal time, and not everyone hired that way gets to stay on and become a regular employee. But she watched me, gave me pointers, and did my reviews. She's so great and has helped me in all kinds of situations; she saw the determination in me to strive to just keep going. She nominated me as employee of the month in front of everyone."

–SALES, RETAIL, FEMALE, 23

Color commentary: Many employees are simply looking for a chance to prove themselves, to show their worth. But their efforts may fall flat if managers are inattentive or unable to identify those with high levels of motivation and a firm resolve to keep improving. This manager was observant and responded with guidance and encouragement, and the outsider who was once a seasonal employee is now a full-time employee of the month. Moreover, the announcement was made in a very public way—genuine recognition for the employee and a message to others about the employee attributes that this manager values.

"We are all human; as such, we all have our up and down days. When our manager has a down day, he will openly ask for help. And when we have a down day, he is there to help us with whatever we need to get the job done."

–EXECUTIVE, MALE, 55

Color commentary: One could argue that this example sounds more like treating others with respect and mutual consideration than recognition per se. But the broad definition of recognition stretches to include the notion of affirmation, that is, providing emotional support or encouragement. That is exactly what we see in this snippet. This manager is attuned to the well-being of his employees and, when things are off kilter, provides genuine support to help get the job done. The manager who displays this type of emotional intelligence is also the manager who does a great job in showing appreciation for a job well done. Not surprisingly, employees who work for such a manager reciprocate when the situation calls for it.

"My chef asked me to make a menu item for the one restaurant in our hotel. I made a streusel for our 'milkshake of the month.' It was a success. My chef gave me the opportunity to make something up on my own and put it out there for our guests to have."

–PROFESSIONAL, HOSPITALITY, FEMALE, 24

Color commentary: Those close to me know that I consider ice cream to be one of the four major food groups, so count me in on the streusel milkshake. But the key point here is that the recognition employees want from their managers includes being appreciated for the passions, skills, and abilities they bring to the job. The chef saw these characteristics in this employee, and that recognition led to an opportunity to innovate and create a new product. Providing employees with additional opportunities is a terrific way of recognizing them. In this instance, it seems to have worked out well for everyone involved.

"My manager personally came down to my office on a busy day to tell me he appreciates everything I do. It caught me off guard but made me feel good that they value me on the team."

–MID-LEVEL MANAGER, FEMALE, 38

Color commentary: What is relevant in this example? It was a busy day, so the manager probably had his hands full, but something caused him to consider just how valuable this employee is. He responded by going to where the employee was to say, "Thank you for all the great things you do at work." The recognition was private and unexpected. The impact? The employee feels great because she knows her efforts are highly valued. The likelihood that she will maintain this level of effort and contribution? A near-certainty; in fact, I would bet this employee will look for ways to step it up another notch or two.

"My manager recently had my coworker get her a report for the campaign I ran. She was praising the coworker on the great job she did on the campaign. But she is not the one who put in all the work."

–PROFESSIONAL, FOOD SERVICE, FEMALE, 26

Color commentary: Uh-oh. This is a huge, missed opportunity to recognize a deserving employee. This manager failed to distinguish between the one who produced the report and the one who did the hard work on which the report was based. Sure, the report might have deserved praise, but the manager's clear intent was to praise the campaign, not the report. What is the effect? The deserving employee is denied the recognition she deserves and instead feels unfairly treated. Yes, the overlooked employee could have figured out a way to get the "truth" to the manager. But the real issue is that the manager was insufficiently tuned in to who on her team is doing what to ensure that praise was properly doled out.

"My manager is stingy with praise. The only time he offers praise or recognition is when he fears that I may be looking for another job."

–PROFESSIONAL, FEMALE, 51

Color commentary: As a manager, showing appreciation for the good work performed by your subordinates should be second nature to you. This manager realized the value of recognition but apparently saw it as necessary only when his own goals were jeopardized. His use of praise was reactive rather than proactive. When that happens, the value of recognition drops to almost nothing because it is not seen as sincere. In fact, recognition offered in this way often has the opposite effect from what is intended. This manager is basically telling his employee that he knows how to recognize her contributions and can do so but will do that only when something important to him (as in retaining talent) is at risk. Bad form.

"Negative reinforcement is his standard."

–TECHNICIAN, INFORMATION TECHNOLOGY, MALE, 54

Color commentary: What is described here is a classic case of active management by exception. This occurs when a manager goes about looking for mistakes and focuses on enforcing rules so that employees won't mess up. It is a very transactional way to manage and reduces the idea of employment to a mere exchange devoid of any human aspects. Someone who manages in this way displays a low level of emotional intelligence and generally has slim prospects of advancing in their own career due to an inability to hire and retain the employee talent necessary to excel.

"My manager recognizes in ways that are the same for everyone; it comes across as inauthentic."

– PROFESSIONAL, EDUCATION, FEMALE, 44

Color commentary: Of course, this violates one of the most basic pieces of advice regarding providing recognition; namely, that managers should personalize it to the employee and setting. This manager apparently does neither, and the employee is probably correctly summing up how all her coworkers experience these attempts: as phony. Granted, not all managers are creative, and they are often strapped for time. But is there really a good excuse for an utter lack of imagination when it comes to showing employees that their good work, good ideas, or loyalty to their jobs and organization are appreciated? As noted above, when managers were asked what they believe employees most want, only 1% said "recognition." In fact, recognition is the second most valued attribute in a manager, following only support and understanding.

"We had year-end personal evaluations and I was asked to provide my thoughts beforehand. We then had the meeting, at which time my manager basically just read my accomplishments to me and reviewed what I had said about myself. He did not actually provide a review in terms of his own assessment of my work. Since I have been there a relatively short time, we have not worked together a lot. But the way he handled this just made me feel like, 'Why are we even doing this if you are just going to use my words?'"

– PROFESSIONAL, BUSINESS, FEMALE, 24

Color commentary: The value of the annual performance review is a hotly debated topic. Many believe it is not worth the time and effort required and that ongoing employee coaching is the best route for performance feedback and improvement. Others continue to see these official reviews as necessary because they supposedly give employees a clear understanding of how their performance is viewed and provide a basis for compensation, development, and promotion decisions. Whatever side of that debate you may take, we can all agree that the episode described above produced no real value for the employee or the organization. In fact, the employee was clearly disillusioned by the whole exercise, and the reasons why are obvious. For one thing, the manager made no real effort to prepare for the review and provided no new or useful information during the meeting. Second, the manager punted a golden opportunity to use the review as a time to recognize and show appreciation for the employee's performance contributions. This is basically an abdication of managerial responsibility. Avoid it.

"I was asked to fill in shifts and was never thanked for filling in those spots. I did it from the kindness of my heart and never once did I get a 'thank-you.'"

– PROFESSIONAL, HEALTH CARE, MALE, 36

Color commentary: All those who enjoy being totally taken for granted, please raise your hand. There is no need for a count; we already know the answer. This employee is one of those extra-milers who is willing to do whatever is needed to get the job done. These are the employees who are great organizational citizens. They are the ones especially known for being conscientious, willing to help, and courteous. What would it cost the manager to say thank you to this employee? Answer: nothing beyond a tiny bit of interpersonal awareness and just a few seconds in the workday. This employee is likely to continue as a member of the extra-miler club despite the lack of deserved recognition because it fits his temperament. But he is now less likely to advocate for this manager or help in recruiting like-minded new members to the team. And, while this manager may not realize it yet, the day will come, and that day could come soon when the manager will greatly miss having this employee around.

Key Takeaways

1. Develop the habit of consistently recognizing the good work and positive attitudes of your employees.
2. Put your deserving employees in the spotlight for your own managers.
3. Note those employees seeking a chance to improve themselves and reward them accordingly.
4. Explain why you are publicly recognizing an employee; this sends the message to others about the performance you want.
5. Provide emotional support and encouragement when the situation warrants; this too communicates your appreciation.
6. Create opportunities for worthy employees to innovate and create.
7. Have a clear sense in your own mind of what represents great performance so that when you see it, you can recognize the employee on the spot in real time.
8. Know who does what on your team so that when recognition is warranted, it goes to those who truly deserve it.
9. Personalize each instance of recognition to the employee and the setting; the impact of recognition will be far greater when employees know you put time and energy into it.
10. Recognize deserving employees regularly, not just when you fear they're about to leave.

TREAT EMPLOYEES WITH DIGNITY AND RESPECT

Some experts argue that this attribute—the act of treating employees with dignity and respect—is simply a sub-element of showing support and understanding or that it basically fits into providing recognition. This is not so, according to what employees themselves say. Our statistical analysis identified treating employees with dignity and respect as a stand-alone attribute. Employees clearly see this as a separate component, and for good reason: When we are treated with dignity and respect, we feel validated to express our opinions and to take actions independently, especially as it relates to non-routine or non-regulated tasks.

From the employee perspective, treating employees with dignity and respect refers to the general notion of treating people well, as competent adults who want to make useful contributions to the team's efforts. It also involves trusting the experience employees bring to the job and showing respect for diverse working styles. It can also be demonstrated in the concern managers show for the welfare of their employees, such as in the care managers take to ensure the safety and physical well-being of employees.

According to employees around the world, this is what to do as a manager in treating employees with dignity and respect:

- Treat employees like the adult human beings they are. This is especially important for older workers; do not assume they are limited in their capabilities or interest or are on the verge of retiring.

- Trust employees to execute their assigned tasks effectively; convey that you believe they can complete the tasks or projects you have assigned them.
- Respect the ability of employees to make good decisions.
- Scan the employee work setting for unsafe or improper working conditions and make the necessary changes to ensure employee safety and well-being.
- Respect employees by presenting them to others in a positive way.

Employees had a great deal to say about this attribute. They made the suggestions below for what managers should not do if one of their goals is to treat employees with dignity and respect:

- Don't pretend to be an expert on a topic when you clearly are not. Rely on subordinates who are better informed and more highly experienced.
- Don't regularly show up late for meetings, constantly requiring your team to wait for you. This shows disrespect for their time.
- Don't talk down to employees and never reprimand them in front of others.
- Don't punish those who make a mistake too heavily; allow them to learn and improve from the mistakes they make.
- Don't allow members of your team to be bullied by others.

My advice for showing dignity and respect

As with the value of being just and fair, we know a lot about the behavior of treating employees with dignity and respect when we observe the failures of managers to do so. Many essential pieces of advice derive from violations—that is, examples of employees not being treated in a dignified and respectful way. In addition to what employees have said about this behavior, this is my advice:

- **Listen to and encourage employee opinions and input.** Employees are more likely to feel respected if you seek, listen to, and acknowledge the value of what they have to say. As all teams are composed of a variety of personalities, some employees may be hesitant to express opinions in a large group setting. Others may dominate the discussion by vocalizing multiple ideas. It is worth your time and effort to ensure that all points of view are heard. The best idea may very well come from the least-forward employee.

- **Encourage employee autonomy.** This may not always be possible, but when you give employees autonomy in problem-solving and decision-making, you are showing them respect and trust. By operating on the premise that employees possess the knowledge, skills, and abilities to perform their work, managers who trust the skills of employees to get the job done are allowing them to perform at their best.

- **Personalize your management approach and encourage diverse working styles.** It is critical that you understand the key strengths that each employee brings to the work setting. At the same time, you should leverage the unique strengths and working styles of the individuals on your team. Learn what approaches work best with each employee and tailor your management style accordingly. Showing a welcoming approach to different perspectives and styles can improve creativity, work quality, and employee morale.

- **Communicate important and relevant information.** When you relay important organizational information and news to employees, you are showing them respect. This may include any important business decisions, information regarding new policies and procedures, changes in strategies and tactics, hiring decisions, and so on. Employees look to you to help explain what is going on in the organization. When you take the time to do this, you show employees that they are valued members of the overall team, that they fit into the bigger picture.
- **Offer constructive feedback rather than criticism.** This advice overlaps with the next behavior—communicating clear performance expectations—but it is also especially relevant to treating employees with dignity and respect. Constructive feedback is intended to improve, elevate, correct, or help an employee recognize weaknesses for the purpose of growing. Criticism, on the other hand, is often experienced as judgmental and accusatory with no purpose to encourage employee development. It is constructive criticism that helps employees grow and develop; it also shows respect to the employee.

MANAGER PROFILE
Mark Casper

Mark Casper started working in the egg industry when he was just 13 years old, performing a variety of manual tasks on weekends and every summer throughout high school in rural Indiana. Today, Mark is the General Manager of MPS Egg Farms, a sixth-generation family-owned business with more than 11 million hens producing 9 million eggs per day. With 10 direct reports and ultimate responsibility for 600 employees, Mark received his company's highest employee engagement score in a recent survey.

When he was ready to graduate high school, Mark wasn't certain that he wanted the egg business as a career. Following his father's advice, he decided to give it a year, signing on full-time at the egg processing plant. Twelve months later, Mark was promoted to warehouse manager at a salary of $13,500 a year—nearly $35,000 in today's dollars.

While he's quick to point out his lack of a college degree, Mark's insights into the topic of people management could fill a textbook. The lessons he has learned and applied over the past four decades have helped make MPS Egg Farms one of the top 10 egg producers in the United States. In 2020, amid the COVID-19 pandemic, Mark's team kept up with a 23% sales increase over the prior year, despite dealing with more than 24,000 hours in paid sick leave. Remarkably, the company has experienced no cases of COVID-19 infection originating from interactions inside its facilities, due to the strict protocols it established at the outset of the pandemic. Dan Krouse, VP of Operations for MPS, says that Mark's exemplary performance as a manager is based on his belief that every employee should be treated with the utmost respect.

Q Why is treating employees with dignity and respect such an important part of your management philosophy?

When I was first starting out, the industry was rather different. Back then, the minimum wage was $2.85 per hour, and turnover was extremely high. We had to scrape the bottom of the barrel for labor, and most managers treated their workers horribly. That bothered me because that's not how I was raised. I also knew it was bad for business.

When I was starting out as a manager, I felt that the only way I was going to get results was to spend time with the people on my team. Whether they were processing eggs or loading trucks, I learned that treating employees the way I wanted to be treated—with respect instead of scorn—made a huge difference in their attitudes and performance. I took the time to train people and help them understand the importance of their tasks, and I expressed a genuine interest in each worker as an individual. A few simple words, like "How'd it go today? Looking forward to having you back tomorrow," or "You're an important part of the team," had enormous impacts on the amount of effort people put forth. Today, when training and mentoring managers at our company, I focus on a basic strategy: engage employees and treat them with respect, appreciation, and acknowledgment on a daily basis.

Q Can you recall a time when your approach to treating employees respectfully was put to the test?

I sure can! It was back when I was doing warehouse management and maintenance. The company would buy old egg-grading equipment around the country, take it apart, bring it back to our facilities, rebuild it, and re-install it. I was working on an installation when one of the guys I worked for decided to belittle me in front of my crew. I'm not proud of this, but I pushed him. Not just once, but all the way back into his office in front of everyone. I said, "If you ever talk to me like that again, you'll be picking yourself up off the floor—and I don't care if I lose my job because of it." Years later, this same guy ended up working for me after I was promoted to the corporate office. I'm a big believer that people can change and give everyone the benefit of the doubt. But after catching him in lies about moonlighting and other activity, he became my first termination. Part of creating a respectful work environment is—and you'll pardon the pun—getting rid of the bad eggs.

Q How has your philosophy of treating employees with respect and dignity influenced the lives of people you have had the opportunity to manage?

There are so many memories that come back to me that it's difficult to choose one. A big part of my job is helping people find positions that suit their temperaments, personalities, and skills. Along the way, you recognize that some people need more help than others. Years ago, I had an employee who was struggling with depression. He was a smart kid, just out of college, but he would go through these dark periods where sometimes he couldn't even show up for work. He clearly needed help, but the nearest counseling center was an hour from the plant. As a show of support, I ended up driving him to and from his therapy sessions. We got to know each other pretty well on those drives. Over time, he learned to better manage the stress that brought on his bouts of depression. Today, 13 years later, that individual is in charge of one of our largest operations. Looking back on it today, I realize that a big part of demonstrating respect is investing effort in helping people overcome challenges to realize their full potential.

Sometimes, helping an individual succeed requires a bit of deprogramming. I once had a processing manager who had been in the marines with lots of attitude and a really foul mouth. As part of his job, he worked with a maintenance manager, and the two were constantly butting heads. The marine, who believed that you get things done through fear and intimidation, was constantly berating the maintenance guy. Rather than letting him go, I decided to invest some time in attempting to de-goober the processing manager of some of the bad habits he'd picked up in the military. It took some time—talking to him about how to treat people, how to listen, and how to influence people positively rather than jamming things down their throats. Eventually, he discovered that treating people with respect earned him more respect and better results. Today, that one-time marine is the general manager at a leading egg processing company.

Q What advice can you offer managers who are looking for ways to get more out of the people they manage?

My advice is pretty simple: As a manager, there will never be any shortage of things on your to-do list. But no matter how busy you are, don't forget to spend the few seconds it takes to recognize, respect, and express pride in the individuals who work for you. When you have the opportunity to communicate with someone one-on-one, clear your head of all your other anxieties and focus on that moment of interaction, because it makes a difference. Treat every employee respectfully, show them that you appreciate them as individuals, and you'll benefit from exceptional levels of commitment, loyalty, and performance.

"My manager always treats us with respect. She makes us feel loved and compliments us on what a good job we are doing. She thanks us daily."

– PROFESSIONAL, EDUCATION, FEMALE, 49

Color commentary: Okay, let's be real. Most of us have never operated in this type of comforting and supportive workplace heaven, and most of us never will. Realistically, do we always believe that all our coworkers daily do a great job and are worthy of praise? But putting those thoughts aside, think about what it means to this employee to be treated with respect, to be valued as a human being who is trying their best to get the job done. And think about what it means to know that the intent of your manager is to treat you well. It is very likely that loyalty to this manager is extraordinarily high and regrettable turnover almost non-existent.

"When I was ill his consistent calls and care were amazing. He visited me often. It was amazing."

– MANAGER, ELECTRONICS, MALE, 36

Color commentary: For one thing, it sounds like this illness persisted. Otherwise, there would have been no opportunity for the admired behavior to be "consistent." The calls to ask about the employee's well-being were accompanied by visits that also provided encouragement and support. A genuine interest on the part of the manager was evident in the time and effort expended in showing concern for the employee. It is one thing to think about doing something or to say you are going to do something and an entirely different thing to make it happen. The fact that this does not happen very frequently in today's world is revealed in the reaction of the employee: simple amazement. The world would be a better place if this happened more often.

"She taught me how to deal with difficult children and how to deal with parents during a situation that came up where we were accused of showing insensitivity and racism."

– PROFESSIONAL, EDUCATION, FEMALE, 56

Color commentary: This sounds like a difficult and delicate situation rife with strong emotions and the potential of an unpleasant aftermath. When employees find themselves in a circumstance like this, what do they most need? Don't they need the guidance and support of an experienced mentor who can direct them down the right path? And do so without being condescending or accusatory? The manager or mentor who operates this way is drawing on a well of valuable experience. That is treating an employee with dignity and respect: no blame, just workable solutions.

"My current manager has always treated me with respect. There has not been a point in the time we've worked together that I've felt disrespected or undervalued. We've had tough conversations, but she's always approached them with compassion and respect."

– MID-LEVEL MANAGER, HEALTH CARE, FEMALE, 51

Color commentary: It sounds like treating others with dignity and respect is built into this manager's DNA. The employee emphasizes consistency by noting that respect has always been shown and that disrespect has never been shown. But it is not just the consistency of the behavior that stands out; it is also that the manager was "always" respectful, even during "tough conversations." Conflict and working through difficulties are part and parcel of any manager's job, but this incident reminds us that even such tough parts of the job can be handled in a way that shows respect toward others. Well done!

"She allowed me to use my own judgment to make decisions for my team. Empowerment is the word."

– MID-LEVEL MANAGER, GOVERNMENT, FEMALE, 59

Color commentary: The ways in which managers treat employees with dignity and respect include trusting the experience that employees bring to their jobs, showing respect for diverse working styles, and being respectful of employee opinions. The approach adopted by this manager seems to hit all those notes. The result? In the employee's own word, "empowerment." Being empowered allows employees to operate with a sense of autonomy and control over their work. Typically, the more empowerment employees experience, the more confident they become and the better they perform. It all starts with dignity and respect.

"My supervisor came to me to solve a problem. She encouraged me to think outside the box. When I figured out a solution, I was praised, and her managers were notified of my accomplishment."

– MID-LEVEL CLERICAL, EDUCATION, FEMALE, 50

Color commentary: Let's start at the end: The employee receives praise for a job well done and her accomplishment is heralded up the chain of command. Preceding that was effective performance;

that is, producing a workable solution. Preceding that was encouragement from the supervisor to be creative in solving this problem. Preceding that was the supervisor presenting the employee with an unsolved problem, thus providing the employee with the opportunity to do work that was interesting and mentally challenging. The starting point: the supervisor trusting the employee to be able to pull this off. In the end, the employee felt that she was treated with dignity and respect.

"Our manager does not help and acts as a solo player rather than as a leader of our team. It makes everyone feel as if we are in a competition rather than a cooperative work environment."

– PROFESSIONAL, BANK SERVICES, FEMALE, 24

Color commentary: It is hard to treat others with dignity and respect when your sole focus is scoring personal wins. Focused solely on himself or herself, this manager does not see a need to be helpful to other team members. The manager is concentrating on how he or she is doing, not how the individual team members are doing. This is a huge blind spot; with better awareness, the manager would realize that the best way to look good is by making sure that employees have the tools, resources, and guidance they need to get the job done. Employees want positive working conditions in which they are made to feel as if they are part of a cooperative team. This manager's focus on self to the detriment of others not only creates a negative vibe but also leads to suboptimal team performance.

"I feel disrespected at work when I seek out more training but am refused. And she doesn't give me credit for the good work I do produce."

– WHOLESALE SALES, FEMALE, 40

Color commentary: As previously noted, most employees want to do their jobs well. Based on their good job performance, they expect their wages or salaries to increase. They also want to keep getting better at their work and sometimes realize they need additional training and development. To be denied that opportunity, with no rationale given for that decision, is a slap in the face. It tells the employee that the manager is not going to invest in her, her job satisfaction, or her career. It is not surprising that it comes from a manager who also fails to provide recognition for good work. Not surprising, but still sad.

"She loves to gossip. My friends and coworkers have had hardships. They turn to me because we have been good friends for a while, and they can confide in me. My manager isn't someone they feel comfortable speaking to, but she will pry and put me in the middle to get details and gossip. It's a rotten thing to do!"

–PROFESSIONAL, FEMALE, 41

Color commentary: Yes, the behavior described here stinks. Unfortunately, being promoted to a managerial position is no guarantee of good judgment, and good judgment is certainly lacking here. Unless it relates to work performance or is freely offered by the employee, the manager has no right to the information she is seeking. She also has no right to put this employee in the middle. Who wants to be trapped between an intrusive manager and coworkers who have taken you into their confidence? It's easy to envision this type of manager misusing such information. Gossiping about subordinate employees is bad enough but holding this type of information over their head to use at an opportune time is a contemptible power trip. The only trip this manager should be taking is the one that leads them out the door of the organization.

"We were having some issues with one team, and my manager scheduled a meeting for us with that team's manager to discuss the issues. What happened instead was that my manager, without telling me, agreed to a large meeting with 20 people from that group in attendance; I had to explain my issues in front of this large group. I was very uncomfortable."

– SUPERVISOR, BANKING SERVICES, FEMALE, 35

Color commentary: No kidding. Talk about being thrown a curveball. Who wouldn't be uncomfortable with a surprise like this? Public speaking is high on the list of anxiety provokers for many people, and this came as a sucker punch to the gut. It may be that these issues would ultimately have to be discussed within the larger group to produce a solution acceptable to all, but that was not the deal that was struck. What was the manager thinking? My guess is that the two managers got together and agreed on a shortcut process for getting the issues out on the table. Okay, maybe they had knowledge of the situation that warranted this change in process. But why surprise the employee whose role it was to describe the problem and its negative performance effects? Sometimes, failing to treat others with dignity and respect originates from our failure to consider the impact our decisions have on them.

"What I don't like about my boss is that he says 'yes' to any job offered to us by a client. But he underbids the job just so we get it. He cheapens our value, which I don't think makes us look good as a company."

–SUPERVISOR, FOOD WHOLESALE, FEMALE, 57

Color commentary: This employee seems to have greater concern for the reputation and perceived value of the company's services than the manager. Feeling great about your team's "value proposition" is hard to realize when your boss's approach to pricing creates the impression that your services can be obtained on the cheap. There may be a lot of stress weighing on this manager. Maybe he is under pressure to grow top-line revenue. Maybe this is a slow period and keeping the team busy on break-even or unprofitable projects is necessary. But neither reason is implied here. Rather, the employee sees a disconnect between the quality of their work output and the commercial value gained. The employee sees this as a negative reflection on both her personal contribution and the reputation of the company. And these things matter to her. The manager could easily eliminate these concerns through open conversation with the team. That would show respect and go a long way toward resolving this employee's complaint.

"When I said something, he ignored my input but went to the director and took credit himself as if it was his idea. It made me feel used because the right person did not receive credit, and I am less likely to give him my ideas now."

– PROFESSIONAL, CONSTRUCTION ENGINEERING, FEMALE, 31

Color commentary: Treating people with dignity and respect is a sibling to the two personal values employees most want from their managers; namely, to be fair and just and honest and trustworthy. This manager flunks both values tests: He is dishonest and unfair. He presents an idea as his own when it is not and takes credit that legitimately belongs to someone else. Further, to the face of the employee he showed no respect for the opinion initially offered; once it was well received, however, he was happy to bask in the spotlight. Finally, he could have used the occasion to ensure that the employee received the recognition she deserved but was too self-centered to make that happen. He failed on four employee-centric manager attributes: dignity and respect, recognition, fair and just, and honest and trustworthy. If it's three strikes and you're out, this guy should not only be called out but ejected from the game.

Key Takeaways

1. Value all employees as human beings who are trying their best.
2. Operate with the intent to treat employees well; respect the opinions they offer.
3. Follow up on your words with actions that confirm what's important to you.
4. Mentor employees with the guidance and support that comes from your experience with handling difficult situations.
5. Treat employees with dignity and respect, even during difficult interactions with them.
6. Trust the experience your employees bring to get the job done but be willing to help solve problems and overcome obstacles when needed.
7. Realize your own performance record is enhanced when you ensure your employees have the tools and resources they need.
8. Keep employees informed about what's going on—both in terms of changes in work processes and timelines and with the organization.
9. Handle personal information about employees with good judgment—always!
10. Make course corrections as needed but consider the impact of your decisions on employees who must carry them out; don't blindside them.

COMMUNICATE CLEAR PERFORMANCE EXPECTATIONS

I shared this with you earlier: According to self-determination theory, one of the three basic needs we have as human beings is a sense of competence. The need for competence applied to the world of work is obvious: We need to regard ourselves as competent in performing our work and to be seen as competent by others, especially our bosses. Part of achieving this sense of competence is understanding what constitutes effective performance; in other words, understanding the performance target. Once we know the standards used to evaluate our performance, we can act in ways that will meet or exceed these standards. Along the way, we may realize that we may need to tweak our approach to the work in order to increase our odds of being successful.

But what happens when employees don't know or understand the standard of performance? Think about your own situation. What happens when your boss fails to define effective performance for your role in the organization? And then later you are found lacking in relation to the hidden expectations your boss has of you? The result is higher anxiety, lower motivation, less job satisfaction, a dimmer view of your manager, and, over time, cynicism toward the job. Similarly, your employees knowing what is expected of them is a very big deal, especially in jobs were there is more freedom and autonomy in how the work is performed (obviously, some jobs are so routinized that the definition of effective performance is clear or very nearly so).

Employees worldwide told us this about what managers do to fulfill this important employee want: They communicate work priorities, provide clear directions for the assigned work, and deliver honest and helpful feedback on how employees are performing. They also connect the work to the bigger purpose of the organization, to its mission, and to its values. They also told us that the way a manager communicates is key. What employees want is timely communication that is clear, concise, honest, and transparent. As a result, employees understand what is expected in terms of productivity, quality, and timeliness.

In describing this important behavior, employees told us a lot about the direction they want from you, their immediate manager. They also told us how they don't want you to handle this responsibility. According to employees, this is what to do in communicating clear performance expectations:

- Provide a clear description of what is expected, in terms of both process and work output.
- Clarify the priorities in terms of what is important (e.g., quality standards) and, when multiple projects are involved, the priority order for completing them.
- Communicate how the work being performed fits into the overall mission of the organization.
- Provide regular, clear performance feedback; do not be afraid to communicate how work output can be improved.
- Allow for and encourage two-way communication about performance expectations.

Employees also shared what not to do in when communicating performance expectations:

- Don't review performance with employees only on a semi-annual or annual basis; employees need more frequent feedback on how their performance is perceived.
- Don't make performance feedback meetings seem like an unpleasant chore.
- Don't give employees new tools or technology without providing guidance on how they are to be used or applied.
- Don't simply announce changes to work priorities or projects without telling employees the reasons for those changes.
- Don't over-rely on email communications regarding performance; use a variety of means for communicating expectations and reviewing progress.

My advice for communicating clear performance expectations

Communicating clear performance expectations is one of the obvious and most important responsibilities of any people manager. Given our universal human zneed to experience competence at work, it is not surprising that this attribute is so important to employees. Even among first-line supervisors and middle-level managers, one in five indicated that this was the most important characteristic they wanted in their own managers. When we stop to consider that bosses are the ones who largely determine pay raises, training opportunities, and promotions, it is easy to understand why knowing what is expected on the job is so important to employees at all levels of the organization. This is my additional advice on how to communicate clear performance expectations:

- **Model high standards of performance.** If you communicate to employees that you want and expect them to go above and beyond in the performance of their work, you need to display this behavior as well. Actions speak louder than words. Employees are more likely to aim for that high level of performance if they see their manager modeling that very behavior.

- **Communicate with employees about performance in a timely way, which enhances the performance of your employees and your team.** Failing to provide timely, honest feedback can leave employees not knowing that their performance needs to improve. Failure to provide feedback is also a natural stifler of employees' efforts to change. The reason is obvious; they lack the specific information they need to adjust their approach to meet expectations.

- **Make your feedback constructive.** On the one hand, you should not be reluctant to provide feedback. On the other, you should ensure you are providing constructive feedback on why the performance output needs improvement and how that can be accomplished. This helps ensure employees understand exactly what is expected of them. Negative feedback that comes across as judgmental and accusatory can damage long-term relationships between you and your employees.

- **Provide or reinforce the communicating of clear performance expectations using measurement milestones.** Employees want to know whether their efforts are producing the desired effect. Setting up a system of measurement milestones can help employees sustain motivation and performance. These check-ins serve to keep employees on track and create energy for improvement if they are missing the mark. But relying solely on formal check-ins is not the way to go. Frequent, less formal check-ins with employees can also be a tremendous help. This does not require a major time investment—you can have these conversations in as little as five minutes.

- **Discuss with employees how their work is tied to the organization's overall goals and mission.** When communicating performance expectations to employees, make sure to describe how their work is helping make progress toward organizational goals. We all understand the purpose of our work better when we see it in the larger context, when we understand how our efforts are connected to the success of the operation. Doing this for your employees helps generate the motivation and energy for higher levels of output.

MANAGER PROFILE

Cathy Gatchel

Cathy Gatchel is the Chief Development Officer at the Honeywell Foundation, a nonprofit organization in Wabash, Indiana, that is dedicated to the enhancement of artistic, social, cultural, and recreational opportunities for all. The foundation hosts arts-based opportunities such as live concerts, visual art programs, family festivals, and educational events. She oversees all the organization's fundraising and development efforts, as well as marketing, education, and community engagement. Like all arts organizations, the Honeywell Foundation has had to reinvent itself during the pandemic to find new ways to fulfill its mission of inspiring people of all ages through art and entertainment.

Q What are some of the challenges you have been facing, and how have these influenced the way you communicate performance expectations to your associates?

We are fortunate at the Honeywell Foundation to have a broad and multifaceted mission to enrich people's lives through arts and entertainment. The arts are fundamental to the social, civic, and economic vitality of our community. Childhood participation in the arts has been linked to positive academic performance and to social and emotional well-being for all ages. The health and economic impacts of the pandemic, together with the restrictions on gatherings and changes in consumer behavior, have caused us to pivot in many ways while remaining true to our mission. At a time when we are all feeling isolated, the arts and entertainment offer an important escape, an opportunity to be inspired, and a release from the anxiety, stress, and dreariness that exact a great toll on people and their families. One of our major changes has been to focus on outdoor activities and to provide socially distanced indoor venues for performances, exhibitions, entertainment, dining, and celebrations.

I believe that change, particularly during challenging times like these, brings out the best in us. I am privileged to work with a passionate, creative, and committed team of people who have enabled us to pivot in ways that were difficult to imagine a few years ago. Another example of our good fortune is that prior to the pandemic, we began a strategic initiative to reevaluate how we create value as an organization and optimize engagement from staff, the arts community, our sponsors, and the citizenry we serve. When the pandemic hit, we had processes and a framework in place to help us rise to the challenge.

In any organization that strives for excellence, I believe that it's vital to set performance goals and expectations in a collaborative setting. If you simply lay out goals and expect teams to achieve them, you will fail to benefit from valuable insights and ideas from team members and team leaders regarding what they believe to be possible. Collaboration also creates a shared sense of equity and accountability for achieving performance milestones and continuous improvement.

Q Can you recall a time when your approach to goal setting and performance expectations had a unique impact on an individual and their career direction?

When I first started at the foundation, I didn't have the chance to speak with one long-time staff member during the interview process. She had been with the organization for a decade and wore many different hats. She was fulfilling administrative and scheduling roles, helping with grant writing—a little bit of everything. She was doing *so* many different things, it was impossible for her to be successful. As I do with each of my direct reports, I initiated conversations to learn more about her personal interests, career goals, and aspirations. I asked, "If you could focus on one thing, what would that be?" I'll never forget how animated she became. She said, "I'd really like to focus on working with our business donors. That's what I love doing most." We ended up completely redefining her role, setting initial fundraising goals, and establishing a clear process for evaluating progress toward these goals. Now, fast forward fifteen years. She has been wildly successful, eventually quadrupling contributions from businesses. And, operating in a role that was tailor-made for her, she has become an admired and beloved member of our community. Unfortunately, she retired this year, and we will all miss her dearly.

Q Are there any examples that come to mind where your approach influenced one or more teams?

Initially, several of the departments I now manage were reporting to the executive director, who later became our CEO. So, he also shares credit for this example. In evaluating how our various departments were operating, we perceived that there was a lack of cross-functional communication and collaboration. The departments were operating in an autonomous manner, and performance expectations weren't always clear or tied to larger organizational goals. We scheduled an offsite session to discuss some of the problems this was causing and how these problems could inform our future initiatives, such as building an integrated digital infrastructure for communication and stakeholder engagement. One of the outcomes of this exercise was a change in reporting structure, which my boss endorsed. Equally important, during the process of collaborative goal setting, it became apparent to all that the siloes we had been operating under were inhibiting success in fulfilling our mission as an organization. Finally, this paved the way for us to define specific goals, as well as a process for providing consistent feedback regarding the achievement of these goals. Unless people understand what is expected of them, how their efforts will be measured, and how these efforts relate to organizational objectives, they cannot be successful.

Q What advice do you have for managers who want to do a better job of communicating performance expectations?

To begin with, manage others the way that you would like to be managed yourself. Set goals and expectations collaboratively, but make sure that you end up with clear definitions of what is expected of each individual in terms of priorities, assignments, quality, and timeliness. And finally, deliver honest and objective feedback through frequent two-way communication. In my experience, when individuals know what is expected of them and understand the larger context of how their role affects the success of the organization, they will be proactive in identifying challenges as well as opportunities for improvement.

"She had to write me up for my consistent tardiness and not showing up for a shift. She laid out for me what she had expected from me, how I let her down, and what is expected of me in the future in order for me to keep my job."

–WHOLESALE SALES, FEMALE, 41

Color commentary: The honesty of this employee in retelling an episode that obviously indicts their own poor behavior is remarkable in and of itself. But the poor performance of the employee presumably created yet another opportunity for the manager to clarify her expectations. The employee acknowledges that both the expectations and the consequences for non-performance are clearly laid out. My guess is that this employee got her act together and delivered on expectations.

"Every month the work deadlines are clearly spelled out, and I am able to independently manage my time to obtain these goals."

–TECHNICIAN, BUSINESS SERVICES, FEMALE, 59

Color commentary: Not all employees have as much discretion over how to handle their assignments as this technician, but it is not uncommon in professional positions. The beauty of this example is threefold: 1) the expectations are communicated clearly, 2) the employee gets to decide how to proceed, and 3) the performance goals are met. Win-win: Both manager and employee are satisfied.

"Every time I have an evaluation, which I have every year on my date of hire, she always tells the owner how amazing I am at the job. She points out the positive aspects of my work very nicely. She also tells me the things I need to do better. She makes the points clearly. She's very nice but direct."

–HEALTH CARE SERVICE, FEMALE, 26

Color commentary: This anecdote shows how the annual performance review is also a natural time to communicate or restate performance expectations. Note how the manager uses the review process to sing the praises of the employee up the chain of command, but also note this: the manager points out what the employee does well, identifies where improvement is needed, and is simultaneously both "very nice" and "direct." This approach to communicating performance expectations contributes to what employees want: to be successful.

"My immediate supervisor sent me an email before I started my job to clearly lay out their expectations. Based on this information, I was able to manage my team effectively and efficiently to meet their expectations. We were able to care for patients at the highest possible level and make the biggest impact on them, which gave everyone the greatest possible personal satisfaction."

–PROFESSIONAL, HEALTH CARE, FEMALE, 29

Color commentary: A big part of bringing a new person onto the team is making sure they know what the job is really all about and what is expected of them. This manager got off to a great start with this employee by clearly laying out the performance expectations before she even started the job. This allowed the employee to enter the new position in a great frame of mind; she was well informed and ready to roll. The result? According to the employee, it was effective and efficient team management, high-quality patient care, and a high level of personal job satisfaction for the team members. Who wouldn't want that?

"When the organization went to a new software program to help make things work more efficiently, she did a great job of making sure everyone was trained properly in the new system."

–CLERK, HEALTH CARE SERVICES, MALE, 61

Color commentary: Okay, this example is more about training staff than clearly communicating performance expectations. Even so, though, the example is important. The goal of the new software system was to create a more efficient workflow. But, as it was new, employees had to be trained on its use to optimize their performance, and it was on the manager to ensure the necessary training was provided. This no doubt gave the manager an opportunity to communicate post-training performance expectations. The energy the manager put into ensuring that proper training occurred reinforced the training program's importance and the greater efficiencies expected.

"When I first became a Shifter, my manager told me his expectations. He said to be safe, slow, and steady, not to run to into anything, and, if you're not sure, pull forward, assess the situation, and proceed slowly. I move 53' and 28' trailers around the yard and back them onto different bays for loading and unloading."

–OPERATIVE, FEMALE, 49

Color commentary: I know about trailering a fishing boat and hauling away brush on an eight-foot utility trailer but know nothing about how to do the work described here. It sounds intimidating. No doubt this employee came to the job with the proper training and credentials. Even so, this manager was clear about what he expected: safety, slow and steady performance, no accidents, a high degree of vigilance, and course correction when warranted. There are no contradictory or ambiguous messages here; rather, there is a clear statement about performance expectations.

"My manager would consistently keep information from people; nobody knew exactly why, but it was always so frustrating. We couldn't always do our job properly, and it was not a good work environment."

–SALESPERSON, MALE, 26

Color commentary: Some people are not cut out for a managerial role and are much better suited as what are known as "individual contributors." That seems to the case here. Obviously, a very important part of being a manager is communicating the performance expected of subordinates and providing feedback on how well they are doing. The communications failures of this manager were both common and inexplicable, resulting in frustrated employees who were hampered in performing their work. My prediction is that this manager does not do well in retaining talented staff.

"Deadlines are poorly communicated at times, which results in significant stress and frustration."

–MID-LEVEL MANAGER, MALE, 54

Color commentary: Part of doing our jobs well includes completing our work on time. Employees may know exactly *how* to perform a wide variety of tasks but not knowing the priorities of their manager can lead to a lot of problems, performance and otherwise. In this case, employees are left confused. That ongoing confusion eventually produces frustration and stress. While a moderate amount of stress may lead to higher levels of performance, unnecessary or persistently high levels of stress actually lead to suboptimal performance. This manager is not only annoying their subordinate employees but also contributing to team-wide underperformance.

"When we had to suddenly go to all-online teaching last spring, our department chair was too busy moving his own courses to help the rest of the faculty. This was especially difficult for part-timers who do not have the same resources as full-time faculty. Some of us did find other support, but the lack of communication from the chair was very disappointing and undermined my trust in his support."

–PROFESSIONAL, EDUCATION, FEMALE, 61

Color commentary: Change happens. When it does, employees look to their bosses not only to make sense of things but also to help them navigate through the implications of those changes. This manager's response was to focus on making the changes required to maintain his own expected level of performance at the expense of investing time and energy into helping others make those same changes. The incident is an example of both failing to support and understand employees and failing to show them how *their* performance expectations can be met considering changing circumstances.

"My supervisor came in screaming at me about something I was supposed to know but did not know because she never told me."

–HEALTH CARE SERVICES, FEMALE, 44

Color commentary: No one in their right mind likes having their manager yell at them over a performance failure. Employees want to know what is expected of them and have the resources necessary to make that happen. Their manager is typically the one responsible for providing those resources. In this case, the missing resource was information the manager had failed to provide. This employee's discouragement is compounded by the fact that the manager reacted in a very emotional, non-helpful way. Things presumably settled down after the employee had an opportunity to point out the problem. We can only hope this manager offered an apology that the employee accepted. Episodes like this can leave lasting scars.

"My manager has a habit of addressing what, in his eyes, are performance shortcomings, just weeks before an annual assessment is due. If there is an issue, it needs to be addressed in a timely fashion, not just when an opportunity to withhold a raise is approaching. It's embarrassing for me, the employee, and ultimately the manager and his observation skills."

–MID-LEVEL MANAGER, HEALTH CARE SERVICES, FEMALE, 71

Color commentary: This scenario involves three people: a subordinate, the immediate manager, and a higher-level manager. The scenario is described by the immediate manager, who is also a subordinate of the higher-level manager. The primary issue is the timing of needed performance feedback, with the questionable intent of the higher-level manager an additional concern. When subordinate employees are stumbling on the job, they need help in the here and now, and related feedback should be coupled with guidance about how to get back on track. The behavior of the higher-level manager is problematic in several ways: failing to share important feedback in a timely way, undercutting the immediate manager by surprising them with untimely observations about the performance of the subordinate, and using this previously unshared information to interfere with a planned salary action. It is no wonder the immediate manager feels embarrassed. It's a natural reaction to unfair and unethical behavior from a higher-level manager.

"My manager is a joke and doesn't have the backbone to hold anyone accountable for their actions or the work they perform. The good workers go unnoticed, and the bootlickers get praise and recognition."

–HEAVY MANUFACTURING, MALE, 44

Color commentary: It is understandable that most managers want to be on good terms with their employees but failing to hold them accountable for their performance is not, in the long run, a good recipe for baking that cake. The failures of this manager extend beyond lousy performance-management techniques to include failing to recognize good performance and treating employees unfairly. It is hard to imagine this manager having any long-term success in a genuinely high-performance work environment.

Key Takeaways

1. Lay out clearly what is expected in terms of tardiness and absenteeism and the consequences for non-compliance.
2. Spell out deadlines for work products and give knowledge workers the discretion to manage their time accordingly.
3. Provide helpful performance feedback by telling employees what they do well and where improvement is needed.
4. Start early in communicating performance expectations, perhaps even before a new employee joins your team; help them hit the ground running.
5. Make sure everyone has the training they need to leverage new systems and programs to their full potential.
6. Communicate performance standards and priorities clearly.
7. Ensure employees have the information they need to do their jobs well.
8. Help employees navigate unexpected changes in priorities or the way in which work is performed.
9. Deliver performance feedback in a timely way—not weeks or months later.
10. Hold non-performers accountable; help them achieve the performance standard or move them out of your team.

REWARD PERFORMANCE CONTRIBUTIONS

This is the fundamental exchange, the basic quid pro quo. Employees bring their knowledge, skills, abilities, and motivation to the work setting and apply their efforts to doing what is expected of them to get the work done. In exchange, they expect you to reward them for their contributions. They expect that if they exert the effort needed to achieve the desired level of performance, you will ensure they receive the rewards they have earned.

Employees were explicit about the rewards they expect their managers to deliver. Most obviously, employees expect enhanced financial rewards. Over the course of time, with sustained effective performance, they expect their pay to increase. And, when warranted or agreed upon, they expect to receive any bonus or incentive payments they have earned. But that is not all; they also expect that you—their manager—will be lining up training opportunities and promotions and helping them develop realistic career plans.

This is how employees describe what they want from you. They want you to advocate for fair and higher compensation for them. They want you to invest the time and energy to find out what rewards are most relevant to them. They want you to clearly communicate what it takes to earn a raise and, when bonuses or incentives are involved, to ensure that the performance goals are realistic and obtainable.

But they also see more training and development for personal growth as a form of rewarding their contributions. They want you to provide opportunities for relevant skills training and to articulate a clear career path for them. They want you to provide more than just a picture of realistic future possibilities; they also want you to ensure that they have real opportunities for development, promotions, and career growth. When necessary, they expect you to remove roadblocks to development opportunities and help them build the skills needed for future roles.

So yes, when it comes to rewarding performance contributions, it seems like employees expect a lot. But, from their point of view it isn't a lot, just a fair shake, a fair exchange. When it comes to what to do to reward performance contributions, employees say the following:

- Communicate the pay structure and how and when employees get raises.
- Conduct market research to ensure pay, pay raises, and benefits are competitive.
- When determining pay raises, take cost-of-living increases into consideration.
- If the organization cannot offer pay increases in the short term, find other ways to offer deserving employees a form of compensation (e.g., points to purchase a reward that's meaningful to the individual).
- Ask employees what benefits are most important to them.
- Provide opportunities for skills training and support on-the-job use of these new skills.

- Provide opportunities for cross-training employees on your team; this is also a great way to expand the overall competence of the team.
- Reward performance by giving employees increased responsibilities and more autonomy in their current roles.
- Engage in conversations with all members of your team to ensure you understand their career aspirations.
- Communicate to employees the career paths available within the organization and what it will take for them to advance.

Not surprisingly, employees also had advice for what their managers are not to do when rewarding performance contributions:

- Don't tolerate unfair pay practices.
- Don't avoid discussions about pay or pay raises.
- Don't keep employees in the dark when the organization has determined it can no longer offer to pay out bonuses.
- Don't implement bonus plans with unrealistic targets for payout.
- Don't make employees feel guilty about using vacation time or earned personal time off.
- Don't use a one-size-fits-all approach to training and development as opposed to considering individual development needs.
- Don't regard discussions of career interests and plans to be solely a role for HR.

- Don't fail to support the transfer of classroom training back to the job itself.
- Don't block opportunities for employees to work alongside more senior managers, thus making them miss out on the development of new skills and new relationships.
- Don't insist employees who are particularly effective in their current roles are offered no opportunities to gain new skills.

My advice for rewarding performance contributions

What employees have to say about the dos and don'ts of how managers go about rewarding performance contributions covers a lot of ground, and there are many valid points in the lists above. It is especially noteworthy that all this advice comes from employees themselves. Implementing the right practices and avoiding the wrong practices will serve you well under any set of circumstances. Below is my best advice for rewarding performance contributions:

- **Be transparent about pay policies.** My research over several decades indicates that when asked, only about half of all employees feel they are paid fairly. Of course, this might vary by country, by industry, and by job level. But what I have found to be true time and again is this: When employees understand how their pay is determined, know how to maximize their compensation, and believe they work in a pay-for-performance environment, the percentage of employees who believe they are paid fairly soars to about 80%–90%. Most of the time, it is not the actual level of pay that determines the perception of fair pay, but how you communicate pay policies and how you implement pay practices.

- **Learn what fair pay means to your employees.** You should have discussions with each employee to make sure you understand how they define fair pay. If there are discrepancies between what they are currently making and what they define as fair pay, try to find a way to shrink this discrepancy, even if it means you have to get creative in how you provide rewards. If employees feel underpaid, you may find yourself in a position where organizational policies won't allow you to make up all the difference in base pay. But there are likely other ways you can reward employees; you can probably find them if you try. The effort will likely be rewarded with greater commitment to the job and a greater appreciation for you as a boss.

- **Communicate available benefits.** In many countries, providing employer-related health and medical benefits is a form of compensation; in some, it is not. Either way, employees may not be aware of all the other benefits that are available to them. You may think it is HR's job to keep employees aware and up to date. Fair enough, but if you can use employer-provided benefits to enhance your employees' positive views of total compensation, doesn't it make sense to do so? One more thing: Ensure there are no negative repercussions when employees use benefits such as flextime. You're missing an opportunity to help your employees enjoy a deserved benefit when you mess it up with a stingy attitude.

- **Make a personal investment.** You need to demonstrate that you care about the growth and development of each of your employees. You can do this by assisting each of them in creating individual development plans and by identifying training and learning opportunities that will contribute to their ongoing development. And don't overlook the value of being future-oriented. When you help employees develop skills needed for future roles—those not currently available—you build employee loyalty and identify yourself as the type of manager employees aspire to work for.

- **Put the interest of your employees above your own immediate needs.** Make training easy to access and keep employees informed about growth opportunities. Attending a training program or participating in a learning activity should not be a cause of stress to employees. Ensure that employees experience these growth opportunities without feeling overwhelmed about work demands not being met while they are away from the job. In addition, don't conceal your knowledge about ongoing near-term growth or promotional opportunities that may be a good fit for current employees. Rather, you should be advocating for them. When you are known as someone who seeds other parts of the organization with talented employees, your profile with prospective employees is enhanced, your influence in the organization grows, and you put yourself in line for bigger roles and more influential jobs.

MANAGER PROFILE
Chris Graham

Chris Graham started work as a welder in a steel truss division of Nucor Corporation. Nucor was a thought leader in the area of highly variable, incentive-based compensation programs. Today, as Senior Vice President of Steel Dynamics, Inc. (SDI), Chris applies the performance compensation concepts he learned at Nucor on a daily basis. Based in Fort Wayne, Indiana, SDI is the third-largest producer of carbon steel products in the US, with 9,000 employees and 13 million tons of production capacity. Chris is passionate about the importance of rewarding employee performance. He believes that giving all employees a stake in the success of the business is what has helped make SDI one of the fastest-growing and most profitable companies in its industry peer group.

Our research revealed that the median annual compensation of an SDI employee is $127,630. That's more than 50% higher than the median compensation at similar-sized competitors.

Annually, every employee receives restricted stock units, participates in a profit-sharing program and can receive a results-based 401k match. A report from CSI Market Data shows that SDI had more than twice the revenue per employee of its peers.

Q How did you get your start in the steel industry?

My first meaningful job was with Vulcraft, a division of Nucor

Corporation and a manufacturer of steel trusses. Ken Iverson was the CEO of Nucor. SDI's founder, Keith Busse, was the general manager of the truss plant where I worked, and he reported to Mr. Iverson.

Nucor's approach to business, at a time when others were focused on holding down labor costs, was to pay people for performance. At the plant where I got my start, our paychecks weren't just based on how many hours we worked each week; they were determined by the performance variables, both positive and negative, that each of us had control over. Those of us in production didn't wait for a supervisor to tell us what to do; we found better ways of doing things because it was in our best economic interest to do so.

In 1993, Keith Busse, Mark Millett, and Richard Teets left Nucor to start their own steelmaking company, SDI. I joined SDI in 1994 and was part of the team that constructed our first steel mill. And I've been here ever since. Throughout my career, my job has been to help propagate and expand upon the lessons we learned at Nucor. Employees hold each other accountable and are rewarded for superior performance. Problems are solved where and when they occur; as a result, productivity soars and voluntary turnover rates practically disappear.

Q What is SDI's strategy for performance-based pay?

While the formulas we use vary based on the plant and the individual's role, the guiding principles are the same. Everyone has to be on the same page regarding goals and what drives the business forward. Incentives are based on factors that employees can control. During tough times, we fare better than the competition because our teams are motivated to create competitive cost advantages.

While we can't control market fluctuations, we can affect our sales in downcycles through our daily actions in all cycles. The more direct control someone has over decision-making, the more *at risk* their compensation should be. This can range from 10% of at-risk pay for someone in a clerical role to as high as 65% for someone on the frontlines of production or 80% for senior management.

Q If this idea of at-risk pay is so successful in building a profitable company, why don't more companies embrace the idea?

That's a question I've been asked many times over the course of my career. Most people don't make the proper connection between our results and our compensation. They say, "We can't afford to pay our folks that much." Of course, the reality is that a proper incentive system rewards the company with "found money." If you share a portion back to the teams, you can create a virtuous cycle of ever-improving performance and results. The way we look at it, we can't afford NOT to pay our folks that much.

Several years ago, I was given the opportunity to go through the Advanced Management Program (AMP) at Harvard Business School. I was in an auditorium with 100 other execs, and the instructor asked how many of us used smart scorecards to determine employee bonuses. Literally, every hand in the room went up except mine. So, the instructor looked at me and said, "Mr. Graham, why don't you use a smart scorecard system to determine bonuses?" My answer was pretty simple. Scorecarding is inherently subjective. It focuses on supposed desirable behaviors that are usually impossible to align with measurable business outcomes. With scorecarding, a typical manager sits down with a direct report and says, "Here are the goals and behaviors you need to work on that will dictate your bonus of up to 10%." While these may be interesting variables through which to assess people, there's no way to ensure that the goals, combined with all the other subjective criteria used by managers and employees across the company, align with measurable business outcomes.

I shared with my fellow AMP classmates that we believe managers need to keep things simple so that employees throughout the organization can understand what's important without any confusion. At SDI, we give all workers a transparent, straightforward, formulaic roadmap to earn above-average income, ensure job security, and have opportunities for advancement.

Q When SDI acquires a company, how do you go about instilling a performance-based compensation mindset into the culture?

We literally don't change anything after we close on an acquisition until we understand how everyone's getting paid and rewarded. That's the first thing that needs to be tweaked for us to eventually reach our full potential. I'll sit with a supervisor, for example, and ask them to explain how they're getting paid. Typically, there's a great disparity, with the crew having a far greater amount of their income at risk than the supervisor. The problem is that when supervisors make bad decisions, they aren't impacted to anywhere near the same degree as their direct reports. This is an inequitable distribution of risk and accountability. If the supervisor and the crew all have, for example, 65% of their pay at risk, everyone is in the same boat and equally responsible—and compensated—for success. In my role, 80% of my pay is at risk. If a business I'm integrating performs well and delivers results, I have the opportunity to earn more than 90%

of my peers. This also applies to our CEO. Have you heard about those CEOs who lay off thousands of people but still get a huge bonus? That would never happen here. If we have a down year, our CEO might be among the lowest-paid CEOs in the Fortune 500. The respect and trust this alignment earns from the people throughout the organization is enormous. We're literally in this together as a business. You read a lot about equity in the workplace these days. At SDI, we have a system that ensures economic equity. It's not without complications, but the proof is in the results. SDI has led the industry in EBITDA margins in each of the last 10 years.

Q What advice do you have for managers who want to improve at rewarding performance contributions?

I have three pieces of advice. First, recognize the advantages of an entire workforce that's engaged, invested, and rewarded for success. Second, get everyone on the same page regarding goals and the measurable variables that drive success. Third, structure performance-based compensation packages to ensure that the more control someone has over measurable outcomes, the higher their at-risk compensation and rewards.

"When I had my last performance review, I received a good raise that I thought was comparable to the work that I was doing, and it made me feel really good."

–CLERICAL, WHOLESALE, FEMALE, 57

Color commentary: Basically, this is what it is all about. From the perspective of the employee, a fair deal is one in which the compensation is equal to the value of the work performed. The policy of this company appears to be that of reviewing—and potentially adjusting—the salary at the same time as performance is reviewed. While not all organizations abide by this same policy, it is a common practice. For this employee, the salary increase matched the performance contribution: all is well.

"He gave me a $500 bonus and 30 hours of leave a few weeks ago. It made me feel good and appreciated."

–PROFESSIONAL, GOVERNMENT, MALE, 54

Color commentary: This incident is instructive for at least three reasons. For one, it shows that not all performance rewards need to come in the form of money. In addition, the reward was seen as, well, rewarding. This manager must have known the employee well enough to know their reward preferences and used that knowledge to create an on-target package. Finally, the reward made the employee feel appreciated. That feeling of appreciation is critical to a positive EX and an ongoing commitment to the job and the employer.

"I did a large, urgently needed job that caused me to stay overtime and got it done when it was needed. She acknowledged that and gave me a gift card for working above and beyond what's expected."

–TECHNICIAN, MINING, FEMALE, 59

Color commentary: This provides another example of a spot reward matching the performance contribution. An urgent need existed, the employee worked additional hours to meet that need, and the manager responded with a meaningful reward. We are not told the gift card's value, but it's easy to infer that it produced the intended response: The employee felt genuinely thanked for their extra effort. The next time an urgent need pops up, this employee will be willing to answer the call.

"I work at a call center, and every time someone makes a sale, they get to spin a prize wheel that is mounted on the wall. The prizes are mostly candy bars and drinks, but every time I spin that wheel, I get a great sense of satisfaction and achievement. It gives me reason to keep on placing calls and striving for the next sale. This kind of reward system also adds something to the culture of your company."

–SALES, BUSINESS SERVICES, MALE, 42

Color commentary: Okay, maybe candy and drinks aren't the best way to contribute to the health and physical well-being of your employees, and this example probably speaks more to a company practice as opposed to one tied to a specific manager. But it is still instructive. If you want more of a particular kind of behavior, then reward that behavior when it happens. As this employee communicates, it's not really about the reward itself but about the satisfaction of achieving a goal, the public recognition that comes along with it, and the motivation it provides to keep producing. Note also how this employee describes the company's culture: it's fun, and performance gets rewarded.

"I was once sent abroad to receive training, which was something I had hoped for and been expecting for a long time. Shortly after I returned, I was promoted and became a closer working associate of my boss."

–EXECUTIVE, FEMALE, 35

Color commentary: Rewarding good performance with additional training and development opportunities is very meaningful to employees. In this case, completing the training program seems to have been a prelude to a higher-level position that no doubt also provided greater compensation. This example touches on at least four ways of rewarding performance: training, promotion, compensation, and an opportunity to work more closely with a valued mentor.

"I was asked to take some training on a new problem-solving technique to learn to become a mentor for this program. It gave me a sense of satisfaction that my skills here were being recognized."

–PROFESSIONAL, HEAVY MANUFACTURING, MALE, 56

Color commentary: Managers recognize employee skills because those skills are necessary for producing higher performance. The good performance of this employee was rewarded with the opportunity to learn a new technique and then become the designated trainer of others in its application. The employee's increased job satisfaction is evidence that this way of being rewarded was very meaningful.

"My first year on the job they were giving out bonuses for exceptional employee performance, and my boss chose me for the bonus. I felt valued and validated that my hard work was worth something. I think the long-term consequence, however, is that my boss tends to take advantage of the hard work and doesn't distribute work fairly."

–EDUCATOR, FEMALE, 35

Color commentary: At the beginning, all was right: Good performance was rewarded financially in a very meaningful way. But the extra rewards stopped coming despite the increase in workload. This recalls the old saying, "hard work is its own reward." This means different things to different people, but to me it suggests that good, dutiful performance is often met with the "reward" of being assigned an increased workload. This employee is clearly indicating that the increased workload is not balanced by additional compensation. The manager appears to be operating with the expectation that the earlier bonus is a sufficient reward once and for all time to produce ongoing motivation. That is a misjudgment. What the worker sees is unfairness, especially considering the comparison between her workload and those of others.

"I got a new job with the company in August. I was supposed to get a raise in September, but because I accepted a different position, I didn't get the raise. I didn't transfer to the new position until December. I went four months doing my then-current job without the raise. That didn't feel right to me."

–SUPERVISOR, LIGHT MANUFACTURING, MALE, 31

Color commentary: I don't have insight into this company's policies, but it seems the employee is justified in his disappointment. Apparently, the employee was operating on the assumption that a raise would be forthcoming in his current job. That didn't happen, presumably because the employee had accepted a new job at a higher rate of pay that would start months later. It seems reasonable to assume that the employee would not have been given a new job without a record of performance that warranted that job offer. Employees who are promotion-worthy are the employees an organization wants to keep. So why deny them a raise when a raise is due? The few dollars saved are hardly worth the feeling of being unfairly treated. This is how you win the battle but lose the war.

"My manager communicated to our superintendent that we [administrators] would be very pleased with the proposed compensation package, which in fact turned out to be very small. I was very disappointed and felt deeply that my efforts were not valued. I am seriously considering finding a new career."

–PROFESSIONAL, EDUCATION, FEMALE, 46

Color commentary: Salary increases are important to employees for both financial and psychological reasons. They expect their managers to pull out all the stops to ensure a fair exchange. This manager apparently had little insight to what these employees expected or regarded as fair. He or she may be able to point to a short-term savings in labor costs, but ultimately will be seen as misleading upper management about what the administrators expected. Employees are now discouraged. The likely result is that they will leave as soon as they can find other jobs that meet their salary expectations: penny-wise, pound-foolish. An employee-centric manager will have a better grasp of what employees consider fair compensation treatment, do their best to bring that about, and enjoy higher levels of employee retention.

"I think that my position should be paid more for the contribution we make in comparison to other positions that are paid the same."

–HOTEL CLERK, FEMALE, 26

Color commentary: This speaks to the basic notion of pay equity. For compensation to be seen as fair, employees must believe that their ratio of inputs (in this case their performance contributions) in relation to their outputs (compensation) is equivalent to the same input/output ratio of their comparison group. When this happens, there is equity. In this case, employees believe their inputs are greater than those of the comparison group, despite outputs for both groups being equal; this creates inequity. Obviously, inequity is viewed as unfair, and the theory holds that employees will eventually take action to reduce that inequity. For example, employees might reduce their inputs (i.e., work less hard), seek ways to increase their outputs (i.e., make their case for higher compensation), or even leave the organization, presumably to find a job that pays fairly. The perception of inequity can be avoided through proactive communication. The truth is that most employees will believe their pay is fair if three conditions are met: They know how their pay is determined, they know what they must do to increase their pay, and they believe that better performers are rewarded accordingly.

"I would like to earn a higher ranking in the organization. I had a manager who did nothing to help or recognize this. When I announced I was leaving the department, he then said, 'Oh, but I was just going to recommend you for that promotion.'"

–PROFESSIONAL, FINANCIAL SERVICES, FEMALE, 44

Color commentary: This is a case of too little, too late. The manager's reply comes off as phony. Presumably, the employee had alerted the manager to their interest in moving up within the organization, but the manager sat on the information and did nothing. There are many things he could have done: provide stretch assignments, support training and development opportunities, create situations for the employee to work with higher-ups in the organization, and so on. Any of these actions would have sent the message to the employee that she was valued. That none of these things happened sends an entirely different message: This manager lacks the foresight and wherewithal to help develop and retain competent staff.

"My manager has too much on her plate and refuses to hire someone to help her with her duties. With that being said, the past two years have gone by without me getting an in-person performance review or salary adjustment."

–SERVICES, HEALTH CARE, FEMALE, 30

Color commentary: I understand that managers can get very busy, particularly if they also have their own long list of individual assignments to complete. But this book is intended to convince managers that one of the most important things employees want from them is to reward employee performance contributions through increases in compensation and additional developmental opportunities. This manager had the opportunity to do both but took advantage of neither. The manager's workload could be reduced to a more manageable level by divvying up some of her assignments and redistributing them to subordinate staff. This would allow these employees to stretch, develop some new skills, and gain relevant experience. It may reasonably position them as candidates for managerial roles. With a reduced workload, the manager would then have the needed time to ensure performance reviews were completed and warranted salary adjustments made. As the saying goes, "sometimes we can't see the forest for the trees."

Key Takeaways

1. Match salary increases to the contributions employees make and reinforce the perception of pay for performance.
2. Use a full range of options for rewarding performance, including spot bonuses, points if performance-based recognition exists, and extra time off.
3. Reward the performance you want at the time it occurs.
4. Provide additional training and development opportunities for top performers, especially for those wishing to advance their careers.
5. Consider balancing increased workloads with higher pay.
6. Provide salary adjustments at the promised time.
7. Realize that rewarding effective performers with only slight increases in pay will likely produce resentment and turnover.
8. Eliminate the perception of pay inequity by educating employees or providing additional compensation as warranted.
9. Make sure employees know what they must do to increase their pay.
10. Encourage high performers with stretch assignments and the opportunity to gain new relevant experience.

CHAPTER 4

Practicing the One Key Skill Employees Value Most

In this chapter I discuss the one skill that employees most want from a manager: problem-solving and decision-making. It is assumed that managers are supposed to make decisions and solve problems. In fact, those are two of your most basic responsibilities as a manager. It is a major reason why you get paid more than the people who work for you. Employees understand this—they expect you to make decisions and to solve problems. Here's the thing: They don't just expect you to do these things, they also want very much for you to do these things well. That's why 12% of all employees worldwide identified this expertise as the most important thing they wanted from their manager.

Think about this for a minute. Have you ever worked for someone who just couldn't seem to decide in a timely way, but rather dithered for days or even weeks? If so, how did that feel—especially if the needed decision was critical to your job responsibilities? Have you ever worked for someone who, despite not having a great track record at solving problems, never involved employees in solving the problem, but rather always insisted that their solution was the route to choose? If so, how did that make you feel—especially if employees had more information about the problem than did the manager?

In both cases, and countless others you could describe from your own experience, the manager in question was not skilled at problem-solving and decision-making. Working for a boss like that is simply not fun. It destroys job satisfaction, drains away employee engagement, scuttles the desire to go the extra mile to get the job done, and puts an unnecessary limit on team productivity. About the only thing it increases is frustration, followed by the desire to go work for somebody else.

This chapter flows like the previous chapter. First, I quickly review how employees define problem-solving and decision-making. I then outline how this skill can be used to motivate employees and how it can be used to frustrate them. Next, I share advice on how you can put this skill into practice to achieve your goals as a manager. This is followed by a profile of a manager who excels at problem-solving and decision-making and quotations from employees on their positive and negative experiences with managers. Finally, I share key takeaways you can incorporate into your daily routine.

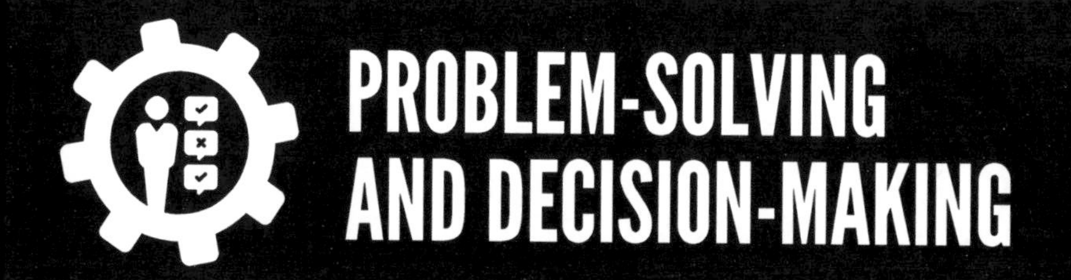

PROBLEM-SOLVING AND DECISION-MAKING

The attribute of demonstrating competence in problem-solving and decision-making describes a skill. A skill is something you become good at doing because you have practiced it time and again. Practice is what allows you to develop an expertise. This is what employees are talking about—expertise in problem-solving and decision-making. Why? Because it makes it easier to get their jobs done, and it makes their jobs less stressful and more rewarding. It builds confidence in the team's success, now and into the future. That is great for team morale, team chemistry, and team productivity. And, when the manager shows employees how they can also be good or get better at problem-solving and decision-making, it makes for a stronger, more capable team.

Based on input directly from employees, this is what they want: To work for managers who can make good decisions quickly. They want to work for managers who can solve problems with good, workable solutions. They want their managers to remove roadblocks that get in the way of getting the work done. In effect, employees want managers who understand the responsibility they have to their employees and are competent in clearing the path to their job success. Employees do want the autonomy to do their own jobs and to do them competently. But, when they need help, they want to be able to turn to a manager who can help, one that in effect shows good overall supervision, management, and leadership skills.

This is what employees tell us they want their managers to do in displaying this skill:

- Make decisions based on data and other reliable information.
- Think ahead; take into consideration how current decisions affect employees, the roles they play on the team, and future plans.
- Involve employees in decision-making; they are the ones most likely to understand what needs to be done and the pros and cons of alternative approaches.
- Make decisions in a timely way; unnecessary stalling on a decision has ripple effects on workloads and project plans.
- Be flexible and open to change; if one approach to solving a problem is not working, be open to trying an alternative.

Not surprisingly, employees were vocal about what they want their managers not to do as they attempt to solve problems and make good decisions:

- Don't agree to something your own manager wants, knowing your team will not be able to accomplish the agreed-upon outcome or meet the agreed-upon deadline.
- Don't avoid deciding because of fear that you might be blamed if the decision turns out to be a wrong one; size up the situation as best you can and be decisive.
- Do not allow a problem that exists between departments that rely on each other to go unsolved and thus interfere with productivity.

- Don't avoid difficult discussions that are needed before problems can be solved or decisions made; don't fail to put the issues out on the table where they can be openly discussed.
- Don't simply tell employees what to do without discussing with them first how different problem solutions might affect them.

These dos and don'ts reveal an important fact: Almost all employees want to be part of a winning team, a team that is successful in getting its work done on time and with the right outcome. To do that, most employees realize that they need a skilled manager, one who can solve problems and make good decisions. Managers who possess this competency obviously provide a big boost to team productivity, but they also provide a big boost to employee engagement. This is especially true when they do two things: involve employees in problem-solving and decision-making and use problem situations as an opportunity to train and develop employees. Managers who approach their job with this framework in mind are the managers who are building stronger, more capable teams for the future. They are also bringing out the best in their employees in the here and now.

My advice for solving problems and making decisions

- **Use an evidence-based approach to make decisions.** Using data rather than relying primarily on your gut instincts almost always leads to better decisions, allowing you to avoid pitfalls. Of course, you need access to objective and accurate data. When relevant, you should also consider key industry information, government regulations, the policies of your organization, and the resources that will be required to implement your decisions.

- **Involve others in the decision-making process.** This may not always be possible, but you will typically make better decisions when you involve subordinates, peers, or other members of the organization. Bringing multiple points of view into the process can stimulate creativity and expand problem-solving resources. When others are involved in decision-making it also increases their buy-in and needed alignment in implementing the decision.

- **Solicit information from your employees about any roadblocks or obstacles.** Asking employees about any existing roadblocks to their work and how they can be addressed is a low-cost insurance plan to getting projects done with the right quality and on time. Putting measures and processes in place to uncover and remove obstacles is the essence of effective management. You may know how to resolve a problem much more quickly than your team. You may be aware of resources that can be applied to help overcome current challenges. There may be times when employees are reluctant to seek your input; you may need to establish this communication exchange yourself.

- **Use delegation to enhance problem-solving capabilities on your team.** Delegating problem solution helps develop the skills of those on your team. You may not be able to step away from the task completely. But delegating problem-solving to others demonstrates trust in your employees and leads to their increased motivation. They will likely appreciate the challenge set before them and over time they gain in confidence and skill. You may still have the final say, but the process can become a teaching exercise when handled properly.

- **Remember Ben Franklin's advice.** When choosing between two competing courses of action consider the technique that served old Ben well. He recommended dividing a sheet of paper into half by drawing a line down the middle. Label one column pro and the other column con. Using shorthand, record in the pro column all the reasons for the decision, and in the con column, all the reasons against the decision. Estimate the respective weights for each listing. When, for example, you find two reasons "pro" are equivalent in weight to three reasons "con," strike out all five entries. The idea is to continue this process. At some point you will see where the decision falls—to the side which has the most remaining weight. This is how you make a tough decision. Ben recommended that you take the time you need to make the best decision. In effect, this process may become a multi-day process. His advice served him well, and he referred to it as "prudential" algebra. Though articulated hundreds of years ago, experts still recommend this valuable process for making tough decisions.

MANAGER PROFILE
Dena Jacquay

Dena Jacquay is the Chief Administrative Officer at Parkview Health—a not-for-profit, community-based health network of 12 hospitals and more than 300 locations in northeast Indiana and northwest Ohio. She is responsible for over 25 departments across the system, with 13 direct reports and the system's 13,500 coworkers.

Q How did you get started as a manager in the health care field?

I studied accounting in college, where I also took a few elective human resource courses, which piqued my interest and later caused me to shift my major to organizational leadership and supervision. My first role out of college was as an HR assistant for a manufacturing firm. I then moved from manufacturing into my first HR leadership role in long-term care and then subsequently into health care. What originally was an area of interest, led to a career of incredible opportunities, not just in human resources, but in other operational areas. For example, my areas of oversight as CAO include strategic planning, marketing/communications, supply chain, construction, and public safety. One of the pillars for me has been a passion and desire to serve others and to help shape the culture of an organization. There is no better place for that than in health care.

Q How has the COVID-19 pandemic tested your skills as a manager in problem-solving and decision-making?

Prior to the pandemic, I believed our organization was rather fast and agile when it came to embracing change. In retrospect, we were quite slow. When COVID-19 hit, thanks to an amazing culture and thousands of committed and talented coworkers, we moved faster than we could have ever imagined. While hundreds of hospitals around the country were forced to initiate layoffs because of steep revenue declines, we decided early on that no furloughs, pay cuts, or layoffs would occur. Yes, we took a financial hit, but we do not regret that decision. It is a testament to our culture and commitment to our Parkview family. We could not have done this without our financial reserves. Parkview has maintained a longstanding commitment to maintaining the reserves needed to continue to invest in the people, processes, and technologies that enable us to better serve our community.

Q What was your strategy for marshalling resources during this crisis?

Our tremendous response began with people throughout the organization stepping up and volunteering to be redeployed wherever help was needed most. For example, we had athletic trainers assigned to schools that closed. Instead of going home and waiting for schools to reopen, our athletic trainers volunteered to help out in our severely over-stressed COVID units. Throughout the system, our coworkers moved into roles that were extremely different from their designated job functions. Many organizations talk about their cultural values and include them on their career websites and on recruiting materials. At Parkview, we have lived our values every day during the crisis, caring for our community and one another. We asked coworkers to be flexible, and they were. However, flexibility must work both ways; as an organization, we also had to be sensitive to what our coworkers were dealing with in their own lives. Early in my career, I learned that demonstrating support and understanding for people at all levels of the organization is what motivates exceptional performance. When we made the decision to redeploy resources, our coworkers went above and beyond without questioning that decision and made the most of overwhelmingly unfamiliar circumstances. Effective leadership is more than making decisions; it is about making the right decisions in support of your team and your purpose as an organization.

Q How have your views on the role of a manager been influenced by others?

My views have been influenced by accountability and what that means in the relationship between a leader and a coworker. Creating a culture of accountability is not about the time spent behind a desk every day at the office; rather, it is about what outcomes you achieve and how you feel about your contribution at the end of every day. Effective leaders hold people accountable for what they accomplish and trust them to deliver without micromanaging them. Our job is to help coworkers with the support, motivation, and coaching that they need to succeed not only in their role, but in life. That requires balance and flexibility in the way that we solve problems and make decisions. It also means helping the team members balance both their personal and career interests without fear or guilt. We can all likely remember individuals we have reported to that did not do this well. Those who take lessons learned from those valuable experiences and apply them to their own teams are demonstrating great adaptive leadership.

Q Organizational psychologists talk about investing in "psychological well-being" in the workplace. Is this what you are referring to when you talk about balance?

Absolutely, but I would also add trust and safety as important enablers of well-being. There is no field where this is more important than health care. People need to feel valued and safe to make positive contributions. If a coworker is afraid to speak up about a problem, this results in an environment that erodes trust and collaboration, which are essential for improving levels of high-quality care, service, and innovation. If people do not feel safe about telling you that they made a mistake or about a great idea that they have, then there is no way to excel as a team or as an organization. Enabling a sense of psychological well-being in any workforce requires effort and commitment at all levels of the organization and it is especially crucial between peers.

Q What advice do you have for managers who want to get better at problem-solving and decision-making to improve the performance of their teams?

One lesson I learned dates back to early in my career. Without any prior management experience, I honestly thought that my job was to tell people what to do and how to solve problems. As my career progressed, including greater levels of responsibility and working with individuals who had technical expertise that I lacked, I realized that being an effective leader is not about telling people what to do, it is about asking good questions. Demonstrating strong leadership lies in the power of the questions you ask. This creates a dialog that stimulates critical thinking and better decision-making. When done well, it leads to learning and growth for both you as a leader and the coworkers whom you support. In my experience, just asking good questions inevitably leads to more creative problem-solving and better outcomes.

"We have patient issues from time to time that require skill and great thinking to resolve. This time, no one was able to solve the issue after many had tried. My manager came up with a new solution that was acceptable and worked to solve the issue we were having with this patient and their family members."

–SUPERVISOR, HEALTH CARE, FEMALE, 32

Color commentary: This employee refers to a difficult situation that required heightened skill and innovative thinking to resolve. That level of skill and type of thinking is exactly the attribute employees want in a manager. They want not only someone who can offer solutions and make difficult decisions but also someone who can do it skillfully. For this employee and her coworkers, having a manager like that produced an outcome acceptable to all.

"Doing a lot of curbside meals with a staff shortage is a real test for our manager. She has to make lightning-fast decisions based on what we have available, like if we are out of an item or running low on lunch bags."

–EDUCATOR, FEMALE, 53

Color commentary: Operational managers are often put to the test: daily, hourly, and in some cases minute-by-minute. The goal is to keep things running smoothly and deliver an on-time product or service that meets or exceeds quality standards. To make that happen, a manager must be able to assess, manage, and react to several variables simultaneously. This requires experience, practice, learning, and improving. That is what developing skill in problem-solving and decision-making is all about. A manager with such skills provides the team with a big performance advantage.

"There was a time we were having technical issues; my manager was able to calm everyone down and slowly work with us to find a way to circumvent the problem. This calm demeanor at a time of crisis, which required a fast turnaround during a short time window, was crucial to our success."

–MID-LEVEL TECHNICIAN, MALE, 31

Color commentary: This problem required a solution but not a shoot-from-the-hip response, and the manager needed to draw on multiple skills. The first was that of properly sizing up the human dimension and acting in a way to lower the heat of the moment so that rational thought could prevail. Timely development of the required solution was much more likely when the participants—who needed to work together to find that solution—had their emotions under check. With that accomplished, the manager guided the team through a step-by-step process to work around the technical issues. As the employee states, the manager's skills were "crucial to our success."

"My manager is honestly the best employee I've ever worked with, and it's a pleasure knowing her. She doesn't fail at her job. She immediately acts on any situation and is a great, quick problem-solver. I've seen this in action so many times that I truly consider her an inspiration. I'd really like to know more and learn more about her work and how to strive for excellence in our field. I say this in hopes of becoming a better version of myself and being able to work more effectively in my career path."

–INDIVIDUAL CONTRIBUTOR, ELECTRONICS, 22

Color commentary: Everyone hopes to work for a manager like this someday—someone who is consistently successful, can size up a situation, and take action to solve problems quickly and effectively. What happens to managers who lead this way? They attract top-notch talent, inspire their employees to higher levels of performance, and serve as a career role model.

"My manager had to clean up a project that a former employee had kind of messed up before leaving the company, and it was very stressful; she needed our help. She was very helpful trying to get us all to understand what the project was and what it needed to look like in the end. She didn't rush or get us overwhelmed. This made me see that she is a great leader and that I can count on her to help me remain calm in stressful situations."

–PROFESSIONAL, FINANCIAL SERVICES, 25

Color commentary: This employee defines great leadership in action: Explain the task at hand, outline the desired output, approach the completion of the work in a steady, non-stressful way, work collaboratively alongside employees, and deliver a successful project in the end. There was no wallowing in despair about the mess a former employee made. What emerged was the picture of a calm leader with the necessary skills to meet the needs of the moment. What also emerged was a sense of confidence that this is a leader the team can count on the next time things go haywire.

"My manager is an expert in conflict resolution, always able to de-escalate volatile situations with poise and a calm demeanor. Whenever faced with an angry customer, she is always able to reason with them and find a middle ground without the customer leaving dissatisfied."

–SALES, FOOD INDUSTRY, MALE, 21

Color commentary: Resolving conflicts requires a special kind of skill—being able to see things from the other side's point of view, sizing up what the other side really wants, providing important information without coming across as condescending, and reaching a solution for the problem at hand in a way that maintains long-term relationships. These skills are particularly important when faced with customers who feel they have not received the promised value. Subordinate employees may not have the authority to solve some customer problems and therefore must delegate upward. They can do this with confidence when they have a skilled manager with problem-resolution skills coupled with the right human touch. These managers are also great trainers, as they model the very kind of behavior they want in their employees.

"We needed to get something done for our customers, and it took too long to solve the problem. He didn't get the team together quickly enough."

–MID-LEVEL PROFESSIONAL, EDUCATION, MALE, 56

Color commentary: The problem here is dissatisfied customers. It leads to a weakening of customer loyalty and a willingness on their part to consider other options. Losing customers due to poor performance not only dents top-line revenue but also damages product and service reputation. It's obviously bad for business, and managers must operate with a clear appreciation of its importance. This manager was slow off the mark in assessing the situation and pulling together the resources needed to solve the problem. Any damage done to customer relationships was clearly avoidable.

"Classifications are not always researched well enough, and I feel it's something our manager should stress more, along with auditing and training staff when shipments aren't processed correctly. Sometimes she wants to be the friend more than the boss."

–PROFESSIONAL, BUSINESS SERVICES, FEMALE, 45

Color commentary: The problem here is improperly processed shipments. This results in expending unnecessary time and money to fix an entirely avoidable mistake. This is a classic managerial problem: What corrections are needed upstream to avoid the mistake in the first place? According to this employee, the solution lies in a combination of auditing work processes, making sure staff are properly trained, and ensuring worker compliance with the required process steps. It is hard for managers to size up a situation and implement the necessary corrections when their own priorities are out of whack.

"She got flustered when trying to make a decision about meeting with students. She got angry and walked out of the meeting while we were still struggling with the issue."

–PROFESSIONAL, EDUCATION, FEMALE, 48

Color commentary: Some problems are just plain hard to solve. Team members may toss many possible solutions into the ring for consideration. During the discussion, positions may harden, and interpersonal conflicts can arise. Priorities may be unclear, especially in novel situations, or there may be open disagreement about priorities. Under such conditions a manager responding with anger and leaving a meeting before a matter is decided is clearly not helpful. The manager's responsibility is to frame the discussion considering the organization's mission and operating priorities. Doing so can often serve as a way of bringing team members together and keeping the decision-making process properly anchored.

"It happens rarely, but the principal thought I had left the classroom unattended when that was not the case and lost her cool a little. Everything got cleared up now, and she apologized. Managers are human; they're subject to stress too."

–PROFESSIONAL, EDUCATION, FEMALE, 47

Color commentary: This manager jumped to a conclusion about an employee's performance based on incomplete or inaccurate information. She apparently called the presumed offending employee on the carpet. Once the subordinate was able to explain that she had been not derelict in her duty, the reprimand was retracted, and an apology was offered and accepted. The subordinate appears to have been more generous in her estimate of the other party than the manager, who could have avoided this unfortunate episode and the resulting embarrassment with a more complete assessment of the situation. The lesson is this: Before communicating negative performance feedback, make sure you have—and have considered—all the relevant information.

"My manager took the side of an employee outside our department. I let her know she was too quick to agree with this associate as the associate was unfamiliar with the workings of our department. She did review the policies and procedures that govern our department and quickly made things right."

–SUPERVISOR, GOVERNMENT, FEMALE, 61

Color commentary: This manager jumped into decision-making and problem-solving with an underdeveloped understanding of her own department's policies and procedures. That led her to take sides with another poorly informed employee from outside her department against one of her own subordinates. Not good. What is good is that when she later became better informed, she made the necessary course correction. As with the prior example, this illustrates that decision-making is much easier and produces a much better outcome when it is based on knowing all the relevant facts. Until that is the case, it is better to withhold judgment and avoid unnecessary damage.

"She displayed a low level of problem-solving skill when a customer got into a confrontation with another employee. She embarrassed the employee in front of customers, which was the wrong thing to do."

–CLERK, MINING, FEMALE, 58

Color commentary: From the account of this incident, we don't know whether the manager solved the angry customer's problem, and we don't know if the employee involved acted in a way to provoke the confrontation with the customer in the first place. What we do know is that the manager apparently decided that in her approach to solving the problem, there was no problem with embarrassing her employee publicly. Bad call. That's not treating others with dignity and respect. Maybe the employee was out of line, maybe not. But the better course of action would have been to focus on solving the customer's problem in the here and now and counseling the employee later—in private—when all the facts were available. Doing so would have helped the employee's development and most certainly made for a better interpersonal relationship.

Key Takeaways

1. Offer experience-based solutions when employees come up empty-handed in addressing a problem.
2. Assess the situation and react quickly, despite the need to consider many variables when necessary, to keep operations running smoothly.
3. Help employees keep their emotions in check by acting calmly when faced with a crisis and focus team energy on developing solutions.
4. Realize that your approach to problem-solving and decision-making will set a pattern that others will model.
5. Recover from mistakes made by others by focusing on the goal and developing a workable process for goal achievement.
6. De-escalate volatile interpersonal conflicts with poise by validating differing perspectives, sharing new information as needed, and helping all parties understand the importance of maintaining long-term working relationships.
7. Pull the team together quickly to address an urgent problem whose solution requires the input and efforts of several team members.
8. Consider that solutions to recurring nagging problems may require redefining work standards, revising upstream work practices, and improving training of employees.
9. Frame contentious discussions among team members about how to proceed with reminders about the organization's mission, values, and priorities.
10. Reach conclusions about subordinate performance issues carefully and only after considering all relevant facts and any mitigating circumstances.

CHAPTER 5

Demonstrating the Two Key Values Employees Value Most

In this chapter, we move from discussing one key skill to a discussion of two key values. Values are rarely discussed in most theories of leadership, most of which tend to focus almost exclusively on behaviors. But values are extremely important to employees. In fact, nearly one in five employees around the world indicated that the two values we review in this chapter are what they most want from their immediate manager.

Values represent the principles or standards by which behavior is judged. You attach a high level of importance to your personal values. They reflect a lot about who you are and what you believe. Likewise, the personal values of others can be an attraction or a repellent. The values a manager displays can determine their overall success in that role. Do their values inspire confidence, reassure employees in times of crisis, and foster good teamwork and morale? Do they bring out the best in others by contributing to high levels of employee engagement and high levels of productivity?

This chapter flows like the two previous chapters. First, I quickly review how employees define each value. I then outline how each value can be used to motivate employees and how each value can be used to frustrate employees. Next, I share advice on how you can put these values into practice to achieve your goals as a manager. This is followed by a profile of a manager who excels at demonstrating each value, and quotations from employees on their positive and negative experiences with managers. Finally, I share key takeaways you can incorporate into your daily routine. We go through one value at a time.

FAIR AND JUST

Almost all of us know what it feels like to be treated unfairly at work. It can be a horrible experience. At first, we feel disillusioned; then come anger and resentment. Our level of excitement for the work dissipates. We are not as satisfied with our jobs as we once were, and our commitment to the team and the larger organization has taken a definite hit. Unless we come out of this downward spiral, we begin thinking about leaving, about investing our resources elsewhere, someplace—maybe any place—where injustice and unfairness aren't standard operating procedure.

At about that time, we begin to realize that probably very few such places, if any, exist. Why? Because a lot of organizations have at least some bad policies and practices. More importantly, almost all organizations have some unfair and unjust managers. If that were not true, it is unlikely that one in ten employees would state that the value of being just and fair is what they most want in their immediate manager.

One's position in the organization does not matter. This value employees want to see in their immediate managers is just as important to senior executives as it is to frontline workers. It is just as important to white-collar as it is to blue-collar workers. And it is just as important to men as it is to women.

When employees say that want a manager who is fair and just, they mean they want a manager who provides equal and fair treatment to all employees and who acts with objectivity and consistency. They are also saying they want a manager who judges employees based on their work performance, not on their individual characteristics like religion, race, or ethnic origin.

Employees have clear ideas about how managers show that they are fair and just. According to employees, this is what they want a manager to do in acting out this value:

- Evaluate employees based on performance, not individual characteristics.
- Enforce work guidelines and rules equally with all team members.
- Allow employees to have input into work processes and workflow improvements.
- Communicate and follow the organization's ethical guidelines.
- Show the same flexibility to all employees; for example, allow everyone in the same job classification the same opportunities, such as working from home.

Employees also have examples of how managers can be unfair and unjust. This is what employees tell us managers are not to do:

- Don't be discriminatory in dealing with employees. For example, don't discriminate between men and women or between members of racial or ethnic groups.
- Don't show favoritism toward "pet" employees.
- Don't allow employees to get by with subpar performance that hurts the team's overall performance.

- Don't punish employees for reporting violations they witness, as in breakdowns in ethical behavior.
- Don't engage in office politics by sending the message that it is more important who you know than what you know.

My advice for being fair and just

Perceptions of fairness and justice are filtered through the eyes of employees, and every employee brings their own set of experiences and potential biases into the work setting. You must take special care to create a fair and just workplace. Here is my best advice on how to do that:

- **Explain your rationale.** You should describe the thought processes behind your decisions, especially those that affect the work and the roles of your employees. When the purposes and motives behind your decisions are explained, employees are more likely to feel involved and perceive your actions as fair and reasonable.
- **Distribute tasks fairly.** Examine how you assign tasks to the members of your team. Do you consider their different levels of skill and ability before distributing assignments? Are all employees given an opportunity to work on stretch assignments? If some employees are always feeling left out and that they're not being given an equal opportunity, hear them out and explain what they must do to qualify for these assignments. Sharing this information is key to the sense of fairness that employees are seeking.
- **Distribute rewards fairly.** We have already talked about

the fact that employees want managers to reward their performance contributions through both compensation and career development opportunities. When employees meet the mark, rewards should follow. Employees have a reasonable expectation that if they put forward the effort and achieve a goal, they should be rewarded accordingly. Failure to ensure that this happens can have long-lasting damaging effects on employee motivation and productivity.

- **Resolve interpersonal conflicts on the team.** Such conflicts are inevitable from time to time. You may need to get directly involved in some of these situations. You may have to clarify or untangle miscommunications between employees or assist in finding the middle ground between opposing but strongly held opinions. This is a time ripe for perceptions of unfair treatment. But no favoritism should be shown in reaching a resolution: All issues should be on the table and employees reminded of the common goal the team is trying to accomplish.
- **Communicate and follow the organization's ethical policies and guidelines at all times.** A code of ethics can reduce or eliminate moral ambiguities by stating the rules that employees are expected to follow. You should make it a practice to review these expectations with employees on a regular basis. It should go without saying that your own behavior sends the loudest message. You show fairness and justice when you follow the rules and apply them equally to everyone. This is the essence of being fair and objective.

Jake Flaitz, Director of Benefits and Well-Being at Paychex, manages the company's comprehensive benefits programs, including the nationally recognized Active Health wellness initiative. Paychex, Inc. (NASDAQ: PAYX) is a leading provider of integrated human capital management solutions for payroll, benefits, human resources, and insurance services. The company serves nearly 700,000 clients in the US and Northern Europe.

Jake is active in health care issues nationally and locally. He is a member of the Business Group on Health Innovation Forum. He has been both a board member and chairperson for two Rochester-based health care organizations, the Community Technology Assessment Advisory Board, and Common Ground Health. He is cochair of Common Ground's Metric Advisory Committee and is a member of the Monroe County Medical Society's Quality Collaborative. Jake is also on the board and is the chair-elect of the Rochester RHIO, a health information exchange.

Q As an expert on employee benefits, what are your views on the importance of treating employees in a fair and just manner?

I think it is important to state that fairness is not a benefit. It's a right. Every employee has the right to feel safe at work, receive fair treatment by their employer, and work in a workplace that is equitable. The failure of a manager to understand and protect these rights can adversely impact business performance and damage the reputation of the organization.

While acts of overt and intentional injustice in the workplace continue, I believe there is a more subtle yet pervasive problem that should be the concern of every manager, namely unconscious or implicit bias, which can lead to actions, decisions, and behaviors that contribute, at a minimum, to perceptions of unfairness and injustice. One example would be a manager showing favoritism to an individual or a group in how assignments or schedules are managed. Another would be inappropriate comments or behaviors being tolerated without repercussions. What we as managers say and how we say it are critical to defining the emotional climate of the workplace and the employee experience.

The Black Lives Matter and #MeToo movements have heightened our awareness of extreme cases of social injustice and remind all of us that there is still much more work that needs to be done. But in the workplace, unfairness can also take many subtle forms and foster situations where employees are reluctant to speak up about problems or opportunities for improvement. If a hospital nurse, for example, feels uncomfortable questioning a medical decision they believe was made in error, this can put patient safety at risk. In every industry, employees need to feel safe and empowered to collaborate and make positive contributions.

We know that employee benefits programs significantly influence the success of employee recruitment and retention initiatives. But most managers don't have control over the benefits their organizations offer. They do, however, have a significant influence on how employees feel at the end of every workday. If a person feels that they have been treated unfairly by their manager or another employee, this can negatively affect their productivity. And in an environment where unfair treatment is persistent, you are likely to see low levels of employee engagement and collaboration, along with high turnover rates.

Q Can you recall a situation that significantly influenced your views on the importance of fairness?

Yes, there is one situation that stands out. But unlike the situations we have discussed so far, this has to do with perceptions of fairness with regard to change. It's a problem every manager has to deal with, whether it concerns the adoption of new technology or business processes or changes in reporting structure. Early in my career, I worked in a strategic planning role for a health care system in the Midwest. Just after starting the job, my boss quit, and I ended up reporting directly to the VP of corporate development. Jim was a retired air force officer, and he had a strong influence on my career as a manager. Our parent organization had just acquired a hospital in Utah that was in financial trouble. At 28 years old, full of ambition but somewhat lacking in experience, I was sent to Utah along with three others to try to turn things around. I'll never forget Jim's parting words when he sent us off on our mission: "The only way you'll get into trouble with me is if you don't make decisions." Armed with Jim's trust, our group—which some called "the Kiddy Corps from South Bend"—conducted assessments and made decisions that were not always popular. But eventually, the hospital turned around. What I thought would be a six-month assignment ended up being a five-year stint.

For me, the takeaway from this experience was that trust is the glue that holds teams and cultures together. Without it, change is slow, painful, and usually unsuccessful. Creating an environment of respect, where people are trusted to make the right choices that are in the best interest of the organization, levels the playing field. The key, however, was that we had to earn the trust of the people in the organization we were sent to influence. That's where communication became vital to our success. Had we just gone in and made changes without identifying the problems and the reasons for change, it would have been perceived as unfair by individuals who needed to adopt new systems and policies. Jim's trust in our group was empowering to each of us. But earning the trust of the hospital staff, most of whom were many years our senior, required helping them understand how they and the community we served would benefit from change. That's what ultimately led to our success.

Q What advice do you have for managers who want to create a fair and just environment for their employees?

I believe that creating an environment that is perceived as fair and just begins with setting a clear vision with specific goals, communicating and constantly reinforcing that vision, and ensuring that everyone on your team is aligned with the goals such that they can make a meaningful contribution. Next, I think it is important to act with transparency and enable open lines of two-way communication. A lack of trust is often the result of miscommunication. Many people may be uncomfortable sharing their opinions, and you may need to draw them out. Speaking of drawing people out, sometimes you have to mix things up and give people stretch goals to help them leave their comfort zones. A big part of fairness is facilitating equity in opportunity. Finally, great managers understand that others are always watching what they do. Operating in a transparent manner creates an echo effect. People form conclusions based on the examples you set. When they see you treating others with dignity and respect, especially in difficult circumstances, you earn their trust that they will also be treated fairly. These are the things, in my view, that motivate people to become emotionally committed to the success of their team and the organization at large.

"He has consistently shown that there will be an equal distribution of work unless circumstances dictate that one officer will receive more by default. In those circumstances, he's ready and willing to send others to assist in managing a particular project."

–PROFESSIONAL, GOVERNMENT, FEMALE, 32

Color commentary: For most employees, a manager is considered fair and just when they provide equal treatment to all employees. This manager displays that value in relation to divvying up the work at hand. Can that always happen? Of course not. But this manager has a "Plan B," which is to send in reinforcements when the project so demands. And the manager operates this way consistently, displaying another aspect of being fair and just.

"Our manager identified and parceled out the different geographic selling areas. The manager was unbiased and fair in assigning us our areas. This process and the communication around it removed any distrust others may have had in him regarding his sense of fairness."

–SALESPERSON, MALE, 23

Color commentary: The previous example was about workload, while this example is about selling opportunities. Either way, doing what is fair in the eyes of employees is about treating all employees equally. In this case, fairness is about having an equal chance to succeed in selling and presumably in achieving the greater compensation that comes with it. It is very important to note the implied transparency of the process, the effective communication of the decisions made, and the elimination of distrust among employees that results.

"When they disciplined another manager the same way that they disciplined a new crew member, it made me feel good about the fair application of discipline. It made me feel as though everyone gets treated the same, regardless of level."

–MID-LEVEL MANAGER, FOOD SERVICE, FEMALE, 22

Color commentary: This incident moves the discussion into the arena of employee discipline and illustrates the adage that "what's good for the goose is good for the gander." Being fair and just requires acting with objectivity and consistency and providing equal treatment to all employees. It may take more determination for a higher-level manager to discipline a lower-level manager in the same way as they would a rank-and-file employee guilty of the same infraction. But if they want to be seen as just, that's exactly what is required.

"Splitting up the workload so that everyone could get their work done in a timely manner. It made me feel she really cares about work/life balance. These moves meant that we as a team could get our work done faster."

–SERVICES, HEALTH CARE, FEMALE, 42

Color commentary: Three factors play out in this scenario: fair distribution of workload, concern for work/life balance, and timely completion of the assigned work. This incident demonstrates that these goals are not at odds with one another. This manager shows how all three can work together, causing employees to feel they are being treated both fairly and respectfully.

"The very time he displayed the policy of being fair and just was at the time of the last promotion list. Even though there were people at the front of the line and due for promotion, due to their relative lack of contributions, the manager took it upon himself to promote those who were junior in tenure who had made greater performance contributions."

–MID-LEVEL MANAGER, ELECTRONICS, MALE, 35

Color commentary: It seems the historical pattern of handing out promotions was based largely, if not entirely, on seniority. In many unionized work environments, this is commonly the case. But this manager follows a different guideline: Promotions will be based on the actual contributions that employees make. This kind of guideline is consistent with what employees want, which is to be judged based on work performance. And it's what causes a manager to be seen as fair and just.

"My manager pushed back when the workload of our team became too great to finish in a 40-hour week. We all felt valued within the group and by our manager. If she continues to operate this way, she has my loyalty and commitment to stay with the company and my team."

–PROFESSIONAL, FEMALE, 58

Color commentary: The value of being just and fair aligns with the first attribute in the employee-centric manager framework:

showing support and understanding. Supportive managers stand up for their employees, and understanding managers are attentive to employees' needs and empathetic when employees face difficulties. The problem here was that the work demanded exceeded the time available. This manager understood the dilemma, acted accordingly, and in the process scored a lot of points in the loyalty and commitment columns.

"One Friday, he let a coworker have the day off when the weather was terrible, and we really needed the extra people to get through the shift. I was upset at the time because it seemed unfair to the rest of us."

–SUPERVISOR, FEMALE, 23

Color commentary: This takes us back to how we define being fair and just—treating all employees fairly, equally and consistently. No doubt other employees would have liked to have the day off and not battle the commute to work under bad weather conditions. The problem was that the performance goal of delivering the shift's needed output required all hands-on-deck. Otherwise, the employees who were present would have to pick up the slack. Maybe there were mitigating circumstances, and the real reason the coworker was given the day off was not shared. No matter; the way this manager handled the situation created a feeling of unfair treatment.

"A coworker made a very time-consuming mistake by not paying attention. Neither this coworker nor the manager knew how to fix it, but I did. I was asked to fix her mistake while already having a full plate. The manager did nothing to lighten my load."

–PROFESSIONAL, FEMALE, 40

Color commentary: This employee is not complaining about fixing a coworker's mistake. The complaint is about the manager not adjusting the employee's workload considering the newly added assignment. Part of being fair and just is seeing things objectively. The fix here apparently required a lot of time, but the manager made no offsetting adjustments in workload or deadlines. When demands outstrip the resources needed to meet those demands, stress results. The manager could have alleviated the employee's stress but didn't. To this employee, it seemed unfair, especially since she was the one with the expertise needed to solve the problem.

"My manager only sees things their way. In a creative field, that is not the way to lead and to keep people excited about their work. I believe you should work together in a way that lifts one another up."

–PROFESSIONAL, FEMALE, 37

Color commentary: Employees want managers who understand and support them. This includes providing encouragement, being considerate, showing empathy, and generally developing healthy relationships with employees. Knowledge workers have an expectation that their ideas will be sought out and that they will be asked to participate in decisions affecting their work. This is especially true in creative fields. If it's only the manager who has "great ideas," how are the highly talented and experienced employees supposed to gain satisfaction from their work? When the job is not what it is supposed to be, there is a sense of unfairness. Managers who always insists on their own way to the exclusion of others' ideas and input are manager who will likely have to do a lot of hiring to replace the disgruntled knowledge workers who have walked away.

"My manager took personal issue with a team member's performance stats. Instead of meeting one-on-one with that team member, the manager decided to call a team meeting to address the concern as a team. This was highly inappropriate and caused a loss of trust within the team."

–CLERK, WHOLESALE, FEMALE, 40

Color commentary: No doubt this manager was intent on solving a perceived problem; give them credit for that. From the description, it is not clear whether the manager did not trust the performance stats, or the stats pointed to a performance shortfall. And there may have been reason to involve the entire team at some point in the process of resolving this concern. But treating others with dignity and respect requires first meeting one-on-one with the employee whose stats were the issue. Such a dialogue might have led to discovering unknown facts and a quick private settling of the matter. Instead, one employee is publicly embarrassed, and the rest of the team loses trust in this manager's way of handling these types of concerns. Apparently, everyone but the manager sees the unfairness of this approach.

"One time my manager was not being professional toward another employee. Instead of taking the employee aside to discuss an issue, the manager yelled at the employee out in the open for all to hear. Not only did it not make the situation better, but it also made everyone that was there uncomfortable."

–SUPERVISOR, FINANCIAL SERVICES, FEMALE, 45

Color commentary: Many of the incidents I reviewed that describe a manager handling issues "fairly" dealt with the just distribution of workload. Many of the incidents that describe "unfair treatment" involve managers singling employees out for public embarrassment, and that is the case here. The manager is portrayed as unprofessional, yelling at an employee publicly and making everyone present uncomfortable. Not surprisingly, the manager's behavior did nothing to improve the situation. Being fair and just involves following ethical guidelines for the treatment of others, which means addressing them in a principled, honorable, and humane manner. Yelling at employees in front of others falls woefully short of that standard.

"After dealing with poor, dysfunctional management for several years with no changes being made and losing several employees because of it, I finally spoke up and expressed my frustration. I was judged and labeled as 'too emotional' and a 'difficult employee.' Instead, the manager should have acknowledged obvious management failures in addressing these past problems."

–CLERK, WHOLESALE, FEMALE, 31

Color commentary: The timeframe under consideration is several years, not a recent isolated episode. What employees were looking and hoping for were changes that made their employment experience more satisfying. With no changes forthcoming, those who had reached their limit and had other employment options left. After "several years" of disappointment, this employee finally spoke up. The reward for pointing to the sources of employee frustrations was to be judged and labeled with unflattering terms. There appears to be no openness on the part of this manager for introspection, only a disdain for those who might challenge their viewpoint. It's no wonder employees regard this as unjust and unfair. Employee turnover is expensive, so one amazing aspect of this story is how the higher-ups in this organization justified tolerating these unnecessary costs over such an extended period.

Key Takeaways

1. Distribute workload fairly and consistently; when that is not possible, find extra resources to help get the work done.
2. Offset extra demands placed on employees by adjusting their current workloads or time lines.
3. Consider work/life balance an important goal for your team members when assigning and scheduling work.
4. Protect your team from unreasonable workload demands made by those higher up in the organization.
5. Consider employees' recommendations for improvement carefully.
6. Allow employees discretion in how they go about their work and encourage their input and involvement in decision-making, especially when they were hired with those expectations.
7. Apply corrective discipline consistently, regardless of an employee's level in the organization.
8. Base promotions and salary adjustments on merit, not on seniority.
9. Get all the facts before reaching a conclusion, especially regarding the performance of an employee.
10. Reprimand employees privately; don't embarrass them publicly.

HONEST AND TRUSTWORTHY

Being honest and trustworthy is not a complicated concept. It is about as straightforward as can be. It is about telling the truth and being the kind of person that others can rely on to follow through on their words and promises.

Being honest and trustworthy connects closely to the idea of integrity or, in everyday language, walking the talk. Your employees know that you have integrity when you do what you say you are going to do. What is your impression of a boss who says one thing but does another? What is your impression of a boss who promises big and delivers small? Then, to add insult to injury, what is your impression of a boss who says these things—in a premeditated way—with no intention of following through? Maybe they have a corrupt value system. Maybe they have no standards for their own behavior. Maybe they are complete narcissists. Often, these types of managers don't last long in an organization because their values are found out, and they either quickly grow up into the adult they should have already been or are much more likely shown the door (and perhaps not politely).

But this is not always true. They can linger. They can cover their tracks. They can be one way with their own bosses, perhaps confident and convincing, and another way with their employees, perhaps willing to cut corners on product quality, service reliability, or otherwise conniving. They may not care about the long-term damage they are doing to the team or the larger organization if they are rewarded in the short term.

What is the result of working for a boss like that? For one thing, if you are early in your career and your own values are not solidly established, you can pick up a lot of poor habits. We tend to model the behavior of those who are supposed to be our leaders. More likely, you realize the disconnect between how your boss is acting and how your boss should be acting. You are disappointed, disillusioned, and dissatisfied, and you are probably not alone. Others on your team, except for some coworkers who might be in on the deal, are likely feeling the same way. How can a manager expect to maximize employee engagement, interpersonal team chemistry, and team performance over the long run, when their own image is one of dishonesty and deceit? They can't, and their lack of values will eventually catch up with them.

When it comes to being honest and trustworthy, employees are clear about what they want from their immediate boss. They told us this is what they want their boss to do:

- Be honest and forthright when communicating to employees.
- Be sincere about your work, follow through on your own responsibilities, and demonstrate that you take your job seriously.
- Ask questions when you don't know something; this will build employee trust.
- Admit when you are wrong; this too will build employee trust.
- Be honest with everyone, including higher-level managers, about the performance of your team.

Employees were equally forthcoming in what their bosses are not to do in displaying the value of being honest and trustworthy:

- Don't sugarcoat problems and issues with staff and higher-ups.
- Don't operate as if you are above the rules. When you follow the rules, your employees will do the same.
- Don't take credit for the good work your employees do. That is both dishonest and a serious missed opportunity to provide employees with the recognition they deserve.
- Don't push your own agenda and in doing so sacrifice the best interests of your employees or your team.
- Don't disclose confidential information. When employees discuss problems or issues with you in confidence, maintain that confidence by being discreet with that information.

My advice for being honest and trustworthy

- **Keep employees informed and up to date.** Employees genuinely want to stay informed regarding the current state of the organization. They have a big stake in how things are going and want to be in the know as it relates to the success of the organization, the department, or the team. When you consider the information needs of employees and follow through by keeping them updated, you do your part to foster a trusting relationship with your employees.
- **Take responsibility.** Being honest and trustworthy means taking responsibility for your actions and decisions, even if they sometimes turn out wrong. Resist blaming others for your own mistakes. When you blame others, you quickly lose credibility.

Owning your actions and decisions means admitting your mistakes and dealing with the consequences responsibly and quickly. Employees don't expect you to be perfect, but they do expect you to be honest and to learn from past mistakes.

- **Do not undermine others.** Do not consciously make yourself look good at the expense of others. This type of self-serving behavior destroys cooperation and teamwork. It is not a reliable path to bigger assignments and promotions. It may seem like a quick jump-start to success, but it fails to consider that managers need loyal employees to achieve lasting success. Throwing people under the bus is not the way to earn the loyalty of observant others. When you behave this way toward others, don't be surprised when the same behavior is turned on you.
- **Follow through on your commitments; this may not be always easy, but others expect you to stick to what you say.** If you are not sure you can follow through on your promise or don't have a genuine determination to make it happen, don't make the promise in the first place. Your lack of consistency will become obvious and will not lead to a positive image in the eyes of your employees. It is much better to avoid promises you cannot keep than to make reassuring promises on which you fail to deliver. That is the opposite of being trustworthy.
- **Do unto others as you would have them do unto you.** Except for the person at the very top of the organization, all other managers in the organization have bosses. Guess what? Just like frontline workers, managers also indicate that they want their bosses to be honest and trustworthy. In other words, what you want is no different from what your employees want.

What you want to see in your boss should be shown to your employees: Be consistent in words and deeds, model ethical behavior, and encourage two-way communication. These are the keys to building trust and cooperation and to treating others with the dignity and respect they deserve.

MANAGER PROFILE

Quan Tran

Quan Tran is the Director of DevOps for the CXS platform at Engage2Excel Group, a company that provides recruiting, onboarding, employee survey, employee recognition, and incentive solutions via a constantly evolving cloud-based platform. Based in Montreal, Canada, Quan recently managed a team of seven software developers who recently honored him with the highest employee-centric manager score among managers of any of the company's three divisions. He immigrated from Vietnam to Canada with his family when he was eight years old, his parents having left their homeland to seek a better life for their three children. Despite their limited means, his parents strongly emphasized education, and Quan graduated with a degree in computer science from the University of Montreal.

Quan's humility and soft-spoken nature camouflage what employees describe as a fierce dedication to supporting them in a hectic, deadline-driven environment. Samuel Coutu, who has worked with Quan since they both joined the company in 2004, had this to say about his unique leadership style: "Some managers use spin tactics to sugarcoat reality. Quan always speaks the truth. Whether he's communicating with an underperforming developer or dealing with an internal client with unrealistic expectations, Quan communicates with a sense of purpose, understanding, and integrity that sets everyone along a shared path to success."

Q Why is being honest and trustworthy important in managing a team of software developers?

These values are important in managing any team but absolutely essential in my field. When you're developing new products, your world is filled with uncertainty. Innovation is messy and requires taking risks. For talented people to flourish, they need to feel safe and take pride in their work—safe in knowing that they're being provided with information and insight they can depend on and feel proud to share ideas and speak up about a problem or opportunity. Early in my career, I worked in an environment where that wasn't the case, and it demotivated exceptional performance.

Q Can you provide some examples of good and bad role models that influenced how you practice management today?

My very first job as a developer was while I was still in college. It was in the public sector, and I worked for a woman who took a real interest in helping me advance my skills. She trusted me to take on new challenges when I was ready and let me make mistakes and learn from them. This was a real boost to my confidence when I was just starting out in the field. When I went to work full-time after school, it was for another public sector organization. My manager had a technical background and appreciated my abilities and work ethic. He gave me challenging projects, but others who had been with the organization much longer were petty and resentful, which made for stressful working conditions. After two years, I applied for a position in the private sector, hoping that things might be different. Twelve years later, I'm still with the same company. While I've benefitted from having great managers here, my early experiences definitely shaped my management style and my approach to hiring.

I've built my team with people who bring both social skills and strong technical acumen. Creating a nurturing environment for sharing ideas and alternative approaches to crafting code has been an important part of our success, but I can't claim credit for our greatest accomplishments. My job is to create an environment where people feel motivated and even compelled to exceed expectations.

Q Can you recall a time when your values of honesty and trustworthiness made a difference in the life of an employee?

Several years ago, I had a talented developer on my team—a recent immigrant—who had trouble communicating with other team members. Initially, I thought it was just a language issue, so we worked on that. But the problem persisted, and I realized that there were more fundamental communication issues we needed to address. He wasn't being sensitive to late-breaking deadlines and sometimes left the office when others could have used his help. These were not easy exchanges for me, but we worked through them. I feel that trust is a two-way street. You have to earn an employee's trust before they'll open up to you. It turned out that part of the problem was having to deal with his children's schedules rather than willfully shirking responsibilities at work, and that was easily resolved with more flexible hours. This employee went on to become one of our top developers and won the respect of all his colleagues. A few years later, he accepted a position at another company, and shortly after that he invited me to lunch. In his new role, he had to manage a team of developers. He asked for my advice, but he also thanked me for being honest with him and for helping him face his shortcomings rather than simply letting him go. Honestly, that was probably the most rewarding moment of my career.

Q What advice do you have for other managers who want to create a trusted environment to nurture employee success?

A big responsibility for every manager is to define processes that level the playing field to get things done efficiently, predictably, and in a scalable way, all the while ensuring quality outcomes. Work is chaotic. Demands are never-ending. But to enable success and innovation, you need established processes that mitigate risks. When our internal customers ask me to make exceptions to our processes, I remind them that our reputations are on the line. Processes are the guardrails of quality assurance, and they should be open to improvement but never abandoned. Communicate your processes and their rationales to employees and customers. Abide by them always, and you'll create a trusted environment for success.

"They had to lay off two people this past week, and during a Zoom call yesterday with the whole department this was announced. My manager was honest in telling everyone the layoff was job and task elimination and had nothing to do with their job performance."

–CLERK, WHOLESALE, FEMALE, 61

Color commentary: Employment security is one of the most important things employees want, so layoffs are a very big deal. When they happen, employees want to know the truth and the implications for them. Managers might be limited in what they can say due to company policy or employee privacy issues. This manager hit the right notes in acknowledging what happened and why. The explanation was credible, with nothing negative said about the exiting employees. This is how you build a reputation for being trustworthy.

"My principal always backs and listens to us. She can be very diplomatic when the situation arises, but we have no doubt she is on our side. She listens when we have an issue with a student, does not jump to conclusions, and comes up with workable solutions."

–SUPERVISOR, EDUCATION, FEMALE, 54

Color commentary: Sincerity and reliability are key components of being honest and trustworthy. This manager is described as always (as in reliable) listening to us (as in sincerity) and never jumping to conclusions about right and wrong. Maintaining such a balance makes it much easier to produce solutions that work. Add diplomacy to the mix, and all sides are more accepting of the outcome. This combination produces trust with subordinates (and customers).

"When trying to meet a deadline required by federal regulations, instead of skirting any requirements, as I knew others had done, my manager not only did what was required, but had the team double-check all reports to make sure everything was done to fulfill the regulations. That made me proud to work for him; because of that, my loyalty to him is solid."

–CLERK, FINANCIAL SERVICES, FEMALE, 52

Color commentary: The chief cornerstone of building a reputation for honesty and trustworthiness is being forthright and transparent. Regardless of how others were matching up against the regulations, this manager made clear to his team exactly what he expected: no shortcuts, all the 'i's dotted, and all the 't's crossed. He backed up this commitment with the requirement to double-check all the work. His focus was on compliance. Employees responded with greater pride in their work and loyalty toward their boss: good outcomes all the way around.

"My manager showed that he was trustworthy when he saw someone on the team being harassed and made sure to put a stop to it. It made me feel safe and secure in my job. It made me feel that if anything happened, I would be able to speak up and the incident would be handled responsibly."

–MID-LEVEL MANAGER, FOOD INDUSTRY, FEMALE, 22

Color commentary: Bad coworker behavior is not new. It has been around forever and can play out in all kinds of ways. The fancy term for this is counterproductive work behavior, and all managers at some point in time are challenged by it. The question then becomes: How will they respond? This manager passed the test.

When he observed harassing behavior, he stepped in and put a stop to it. He made his values clear. Those observing were relieved. They want a workplace that is free of abuse where all employees are made to feel part of a team. Positive working conditions give employees greater confidence to speak up, knowing their manager will handle issues in a sincere and forthright manner.

"Early in my tenure with this employer, I came under considerable political pressure for not immediately solving what had been an ongoing problem. My manager worked to keep me protected and gave me the time needed to bring about an acceptable solution."

–MID-LEVEL MANAGER, EDUCATION, FEMALE, 62

Color commentary: Trustworthy managers want their employees to perform their work honestly. Sometimes that means making special provisions. That was the case here—an ongoing problem that had resisted resolution had now bubbled up to the attention of the higher-ups, who wanted an immediate fix. But if the problem had persisted over a long period of time, it also followed that a reliable solution was going to take some time to develop. The manager needed to provide the right ingredients to produce a solution: time and protection. It was the right thing to do and earned the trust and confidence of the employee caught in the middle.

"After six months of working at a store of a national pizza chain, I had to leave the company to take care of some very serious family problems which required me to relocate. My manager told me that I would have a spot at the store if I ever wanted it back, and after the family issues were taken care of literally six to seven months later, he gave me my position back with a raise."

–SUPERVISOR, FOOD INDUSTRY, FEMALE, 19

Color commentary: In everyday work life, a manager acts with integrity when they do what they say they are going to do. No doubt, the manager would not have promised to re-hire this employee unless she had proven to be a good worker. The important point is that the manager followed through on the promise. Not only that; he even sweetened the deal with a raise.

"My manager denied that she had asked an employee to do a specific task that did not go well and then did not take the blame. I am now careful to verify everything by email and save all communications with her."

–SUPERVISOR, EDUCATION, FEMALE, 58

Color commentary: This manager lied to avoid taking blame for a poor performance outcome for which she was responsible. Maybe she fooled her own boss, but she did not fool her team. This is the opposite of being honest and forthright and acting with integrity. This employee now handles communication with the boss by carefully documenting and saving all written communication with her: what a waste of time and energy! This is not the kind of boss employees want.

"He just reveals details of a coworker's situation that he probably should not. While he's using them as an example to teach, he is also gossiping about them and their situation. This tends to leave a bad taste in my mouth and makes me wonder what he tells others about me and how I've handled situations."

–PROFESSIONAL, EDUCATION, FEMALE, 28

Color commentary: You won't build a record as trustworthy when others who have taken you into confidence about a personal matter later learn that you have broken that trust by sharing your personal details with others. Maybe the manager's intent was not malicious, and he was only trying to make his teaching examples more realistic. But even if that is true, what poor judgment he shows! Not only does he violate the basic rules of trust, but others also suspect in advance that he will do the same to them behind their backs. This illustrates how effective within-team communication shuts down from fear of embarrassment while mistrust of intentions spirals upward.

"Supervisor lied about sending additional help when we were short an employee."

–SUPERVISOR, MALE, 43

Color commentary: The problem was understaffing. The solution was to assemble more workers to get the job done on time. That was the supervisor's job. The supervisor did not come through despite the promise made. An expectation was raised but never fulfilled. And there was no explanation—legitimate or otherwise—for failing to send the needed additional workers. This represents a breakdown in two of the attributes employees most want from their managers: provide support and understanding and be honest and trustworthy. What confidence can these workers have in any promises this supervisor makes?

"There was a time that my manager threw me under the bus after I had a pre-meeting with her to review my upcoming presentation. She knew what was in it and signed off on it. When the presentation was made as agreed to a large group, she poked holes in it in front of everyone."

–SUPERVISOR, FOOD INDUSTRY, FEMALE, 30

Color commentary: This incident also shows the close connection between being supportive and understanding and being honest and trustworthy. But there are two additional employee-centric manager attributes on which this manager fell short—treating an employee with dignity and respect and communicating clear performance expectations. This employee sought out the manager's help. A supportive manager provides help when requested. An honest and trustworthy manager is forthright, transparent, and sincere. A manager who communicates clear performance expectations is timely in providing direct and honest feedback. A manager who treats employees with dignity and respect does not willfully and publicly embarrass an employee to shine the light on their own superior knowledge and experience.

"Our manager hired several nurses who are sponsored by the state and are paid three times what we are paid for doing the same job that we have been doing since the pandemic started. (I work on a COVID-19 unit as a nurse.) We repeatedly asked for a raise or some sort of compensation for our work, but we weren't given anything until several employees started leaving and going to other jobs that paid more. I wish my manager had come to his staff first and tried to work and get us more compensation rather than allowing most of the nurses to leave."

–PROFESSIONAL, HEALTH CARE, FEMALE, 25

Color commentary: Three of the most important attributes that employees want from their managers are lacking in this scenario: being fair and just, being honest and trustworthy, and rewarding performance contributions. This manager could and should have known that the permanent staff would resent being significantly underpaid in comparison to the state-provided nurses. The demands of the pandemic may have necessitated this inequity in the short run, but the manager could also have done more to reward the permanent staff with bonuses or non-permanent pay increases. After all, working conditions were the same for all. These failures led to staff defections, making a difficult situation even worse. The bad feelings and resulting defections were avoidable; the situation demanded forthright and transparent communication coupled with successful advocacy for fairer compensation.

"She will promise me more hours after I talk with her and then acts like she forgot. This has happened multiple times. She is understanding of things like taking time off due to poor health, but only if she doesn't have to really help or pay me. She also does not wear the workplace dress code herself."

–SERVICES, RESTAURANT, MALE, 26

Color commentary: Once again, the essence of being honest and trustworthy involves sincerity, reliability, and integrity. To be seen as acting with integrity, one must follow through on promises made. To be seen as reliable, one must be consistent. To be seen as sincere, one must be genuine and avoid hypocrisy. Clearly, this manager falls short on the honest and trustworthy attribute. She also does not lead by example but rather seems primarily interested in her own well-being and advantages gained.

Key Takeaways

1. Communicate difficult messages in a credible, logical, and forthright way.
2. Listen with sincerity and an absence of bias; before drawing conclusions, make sure to hear and weigh both sides of a disagreement.
3. Demonstrate your own commitment to meet and exceed performance requirements, knowing that your actions speak louder than your words.
4. State your values regarding appropriate interpersonal behavior clearly; intervene directly to address staff mistreatment.
5. Communicate honestly about what's required to get a job done properly; protect your employees from unreasonable deadlines.
6. Display integrity by doing what you say you are going to do.
7. Accept responsibility for poor performance when you are its cause; don't project the blame onto others.
8. Hold in confidence information given you in confidence; don't betray the trust of others.
9. Provide direct and honest performance feedback to an individual employee in a private setting; treat that person with dignity and respect.
10. Hold yourself to the same standards to which you hold others and give others the same benefit of the doubt you give yourself.

CHAPTER 6

Three Actions You Can Take Today to Become an Employee-Centric Manager

Chapter 1 listed nine reasons you should read this book. Do you remember Reason 8? It stated that how managers are rated on the eight employee-centric manager attributes fundamentally determines their overall managerial effectiveness ratings. In my discussion of Reason 8, I shared with you that 67% of a manager's perceived overall effectiveness could be explained by how they are rated on the eight ECM attributes. I explained this in these words: **If you rate highly on these eight ECM attributes, you rate highly on overall performance.**

The statistical technique used in creating this knowledge, regression analysis, also tells us *which* attributes have the *most* impact on a manager's overall performance rating.

Dare to guess? How a manager shows up on these three attributes most influence employees' views of their manager's overall performance:

- **Listen:** As in, "My manager is an effective listener."
- **Make good decisions:** As in, "My manager displays competence in making day-to-day work decisions."
- **Recognize:** As in, "My manager provides me with praise or recognition for doing good work."

This list consists of two behaviors and one skill. Listening is obviously a behavior; it is a subset of support and understanding. Naturally, it is hard to understand employees if you don't listen to them. The other behavior is recognizing employees for their good work and the other positive contributions they make to the team and to the organization. Making good decisions is the skill on this very brief list. All along, we have emphasized that a skill is a practiced behavior; it is practice that produces expertise. The analysis reveals that the expertise managers show in problem-solving and decision-making (not surprisingly) has an enormous influence on how employees rate their overall effectiveness.

So, if you want to enhance your status as an employee-centric manager, what better place to start than with the attributes that most influence overall performance? Let's take a quick look at each of these three sure pathways to boosting your effectiveness.

Listen

Listen. To listen connects with the understanding part of the support and understanding attribute. A couple of things are worth remembering. First, support and understanding is by far the most frequently identified attribute employees want in their immediate manager; 26% of the world's employees stated this. In fact, this percentage is twice the size of the next attribute on the list. Second, managers generally underestimate the importance of listening to and supporting employees. Recall that in the survey of managers, only 16% believe that support and understanding are what employees most want from them. This gap represents a significant disconnect in the understanding managers have of their employees. Managers have more work to do when it comes to listening to employees. So, as it relates to listening, what do employees really want from managers? They want them to:

- Be available and accessible. Sure, managers are busy, but it is virtually impossible for a manager to be a good listener if they are never around, can't be found, or are otherwise inaccessible. Unfortunately, when managers are routinely unavailable, it tells employees that they, or the work they are doing, are not all that important. They feel disrespected.

- Listen to employee concerns with the energy and attention needed to genuinely identify with where they are coming from. Employees want managers to be empathetic and can detect when they are play-acting as opposed to truly listening for understanding.

- Follow through on concerns brought to their attention. Part of listening and being empathetic is following through with a supportive response, an action that genuinely addresses the concerns raised. It is of little value to employees to have a manager put on a show of empathy but fail to follow through.
- Seek their input on important decisions affecting their work or on how to solve a work-related problem. (After all, employees may be better informed or more experienced than their manager.) This is a more proactive form of listening and communicates respect for employees' skills and abilities. It is also likely to produce better work outcomes.
- Get to know their employees sufficiently well so that they understand their current capabilities, their training and development needs, and their goals, including their career goals.

Can you do these things? Is there any reason you can't implement these practices today? Maybe you already are doing some or all these things but need to hit the refresh button on your approach. Either way, it is what your employees want from you and what will make you a better manager.

Make good decisions

Make good decisions. Worldwide, 12% of employees indicated this was what they most wanted from their manager, the same percentage as among workers in the United States. Interestingly, in my survey of US managers, 19% indicated that they believed this is what employees most wanted from them. Obviously, US managers are plugged into the significance of this managerial attribute, even though they may overestimate how well they display it.

As we have noted all along, it is not simply that employees want managers who make decisions. They want managers who make good decisions; that is, managers who are competent decision-makers and problem-solvers. To be more specific, this is what employees really want from their managers:

- Make decisions in a timely way. Obviously, difficult decisions that relate to more complex issues may require more time, and employees understand that. But a lot of decisions managers make are not of that kind. Employees see a failure to make timely decisions as a roadblock to their own success. It is a source of frustration and vexation. Talented employees who have other employment opportunities may jump ship when they have concluded that their manager lacks what it takes to make the necessary decisions. Who wants to wait around and see their own skills decline and their motivation dissipate while their manager dithers?

- Make decisions based on a rational, data-based approach. This is not to say there is no place for gut instinct, but in general, most decisions that are based on available evidence—valid data, reliable information—produce better outcomes. The basic idea is to assemble the information needed, size up the situation, and proceed.

- Involve employees in decision-making and problem-solving. This produces a whole host of positive outcomes. Decisions based on employee input are often better decisions because their point of view as informed others is taken into consideration. Job satisfaction increases because employees gain an increased sense of accomplishment from their work, and their involvement also causes them to feel more respected. Agreement among team members as to the right course of action is increased when employees are involved from the outset. The flipside is also relevant: Resistance to implementing a decision is reduced when employees participate in the decision-making process.
- Think through the implications of their decisions. This may be a counterbalance to the first suggestion. Yes, your employees want timely decisions whenever possible, but they also want you to consider the implications of your decisions, especially regarding the match of people to tasks, the re-ordering of priorities, and the availability of resources that might be needed to implement a decision.
- To be flexible and learn from experience. You may come to realize that the chosen approach is not really working. It happens. The question is: What do you do next? Out of stubbornness, do you stick with a plan that is clearly suboptimal? Or, do you adjust your approach based on what

you have learned to date? Employees don't expect that you will always make perfect decisions. What they *do* expect is that when a past decision is clearly shown to be a loser, you will adapt and a select a winner instead.

Can you do these things? Is there any reason you can't implement these practices today? Maybe you already are doing some or all these things but need to hit the refresh button on your approach. Either way, it is what your employees want from you and what will make you a better manager.

Recognize

Recognize. Again, recognition is something that can cost so little to the manager and mean so much to the employee. I have also reviewed with you that managers wildly underestimate the importance of recognition to employees. Worldwide, recognition is the second on the list of most frequently identified attributes employees want in their managers. Yet, in a survey of a representative sample of managers in the United States, only 1% chose recognition as what they believed employees most want from them. This speaks to an utter lack of awareness among managers as to what motivates employees to work harder, perform better, and stay longer.

Recognition is not the same thing as reward. Recognition is a matter of the heart; reward is a matter of the wallet. Recognition is about employees feeling appreciated for the contributions they make. It is psychological in nature—the need to feel and be esteemed by others at work, most importantly by their manager.

When it comes to being recognized, this is what employees really want from their managers:

- An honest and sincere "thank-you" for working hard, staying late, busting through obstacles, and going the extra mile to get the job done. You don't like being taken for granted; neither do your employees.
- Real-time recognition: that is, when their performance is worthy of praise, employees want appreciation in the here and now, when the behavior or performance that warrants recognition

occurred. Waiting to provide deserved recognition until some previously scheduled one-on-one meeting or semi-annual or annual performance review session is the wrong way to think about this. It simply won't mean as much and won't feel as genuine when it does not happen in real time.

- Recognition that is tailored to the individual employee. We are all different, which means we do not all like to be recognized in the same way. Employees want managers to invest the time and energy to get to know them well enough so that they can recognize employees in the way they prefer to be recognized.
- Frequent recognition—not in an insincere way, but genuinely. Employees don't want to be recognized so frequently that it becomes meaningless, but at the same time they don't want managers to be overly stingy in recognizing their good work, efforts, and commitment to getting the job done. Remember, all it takes is your awareness of the importance of what they want and enough motivation to make it happen.
- Recognition that is specific to the behavior or performance under consideration. If you want to see this behavior or level of performance more frequently in the future, make sure your employees know specifically what it is about their work that you appreciate. This is simply Skinner's law of reinforcement: You will get what you positively reinforce.

Can you do these things? Is there any reason you can't implement these practices today? Maybe you already are doing some or all these things but need to hit the "refresh" button on your approach. Either way, it is what your employees want from you and what will make you a better manager.

In conclusion, most definitions of the role of a manager include terms like planning, organizing, leading, and controlling. What's missing and vital for effectiveness in the modern workplace is the role of the manager in creating a great employee experience, one that enables, motivates, and engages employees to positively influence employee, team, and organizational performance. While the above three attributes have the most impact on a manager's overall performance rating, mastering all eight attributes that employees want in a manager is the goal. Doing so helps you unleash the discretionary effort of your employees to improve a broad array of business metrics, including customer service ratings, team productivity ratios, and bottom-line financial results.

The wisdom of this book is that it is entirely based on the voice of the employee. The book provides the most comprehensive analysis to date of what employees want from their manager, presented with 90 easy-to-apply "do and don't" tips, 40 best practice recommendations, 8 successful manager profiles, and 96 quotes from employees on their positive and negative experiences with managers. I am confident that if you become proficient in these employee-centric manager attributes, you will achieve heightened success as a people manager and go on to achieve greater rewards and growth opportunities.

I wish you the very best in the next steps of your career as an employee-centric manager.

Appendix 1

Creating the Employee-Centric Manager Taxonomy

The pattern for analyzing the responses to the question, "As an employee, what is the most important thing you want from your direct immediate manager?" was established in developing my earlier book, *RESPECT: Delivering Results by Giving Employees What They Really Want*. As with *RESPECT*, the goal for this analysis was clear: We want to use highly defensible, scientific procedures for boiling down a massive amount of qualitative data. Qualitative simply means data that come in words; our data were *written responses* from those who answered the open-ended question about their managers.

There are challenges in qualitative data analysis; the primary concern is that it relies on a subjective coding process. We all have our own filters and perspectives on things we experience in life, and we carry those perspectives into how we analyze qualitative data. To minimize this influence, we hired 20 data analysts who sorted the written responses into categories. To make sure we were doing this in a valid way, we relied on a two-phase process: an initial sort and a retranslation sort.

When all was said and done, we had 23 different perspectives on the data—those of the 20 trained sorters and those of three PhD-level researchers. This allowed us to account for agreement and disagreement among perspectives. We checked the accuracy of the sorting process three separate times.

The Initial Sample

We initially surveyed 32,800 workers from 27 countries around the world: Argentina, Australia, Brazil, Canada, China, Denmark, Finland, France, Germany, India, Indonesia, Italy, Japan, Mexico, the Netherlands, Qatar, Russian Federation, Saudi Arabia, Spain, South Africa, South Korea, Sweden, Switzerland, Turkey, the United Arab Emirates, the United Kingdom, and the United States. From this base of information, we drew a stratified random sample of responses from each country, producing a final dataset of 3,072 responses.

All of the responses provided in a language other than English were first translated into English. The data were cleaned, meaning we removed all irrelevant information (for example, when responses did not answer the question). We assigned 10 sorters to the initial sorting task and 10 to the retranslation sorting task.

The Initial Sort

In the initial sort, the sorters read the comments and created a preliminary set of response categories. They then re-read each comment and carefully assigned the comment to an established category; they also revised category names to ensure that they properly summarized the comments in the category.

We collected the work product of all 10 sorters and combined their results. We then conducted a principal component analysis (PCA) that examined the amount of agreement among the sorters. The PCA was used to extract statistically derived component categories. After discussion and review among the three lead researchers, we arrived at an eight-factor solution or taxonomy.

The Retranslation Sort

In the retranslation sort, sorters assigned a subsample of responses to the initially defined set of categories. The subsample was comprised of different responses than those used in the initial sort.

The retranslation sort of the subsample supported the original taxonomy, meaning that sorters agreed on the placement of comments into categories. This allowed us to continue with the coding process. When the process was complete, all but 2% of the comments could be placed into one of the eight categories that employees consider the most important thing they want from their immediate manager.

Finalizing the Taxonomy

Finalizing the taxonomy involved ensuring that the 2% of comments that could not be categorized into the taxonomy were indeed outliers; they were. We also reviewed category names to ensure they properly reflected the contents of each category. As the senior researcher, I took responsibility for final category naming. The final taxonomy is presented in Table A1.1 below.

Table A1.1

Employee-Centric Manager Attribute Categories and Subcategories

Category	Subcategory	Attribute
1. Support and Understanding	1a. Support	Be present and accessible
		Provide help and support in daily activities
		Be encouraging
		Stand up for employees
		Follow through on employee concerns/issues
	1b. Understanding	Listen and be understanding
		Be considerate and friendly
		Be attentive to employees' needs, difficulties, responsibilities, etc.
		Show empathy
		Develop healthy relationships with employees
2. Recognition		Compliment and praise good work
		Show affirmation and appreciation
		Give credit for good ideas
		Recognize loyalty to the job and organization
		Recognize both the team and individuals
		Personalize recognition
		Recognize efforts, passion, skills, abilities, and achievements
3. Dignity and Respect		Treat employees with dignity and respect
		Demonstrate humane and good treatment
		Show respect for diverse working styles
		Trust the experience employees bring
		Be respectful of employee opinions

Category	Subcategory	Behavior
4. Clear Performance Expectations		Provide clear directions and guidance
		Communicate priorities
		Provide direct and honest feedback on performance
		Be timely with communication
		Be clear, honest, concise, and transparent when communicating
		Connect the work to the organization's mission/values
5. Reward Performance Contributions	5a. Financial Rewards	Advocate for fair compensation
		Ask employees what rewards are most relevant to them
		Provide better and/or fair financial compensation, benefits, and/or bonuses
		Communicate how financial rewards are determined
		Ensure bonuses/raises are obtainable
		Ensure benefits are comparable to the market/industry
	5b. Training and Development Rewards	Provide opportunities for relevant training
		Create clear career paths for employees
		Provide opportunities for career development, promotions, and professional growth
		Remove any roadblocks prohibiting opportunities for development
		Provide opportunities to develop skills that will be required for future roles
6. Problem-Solving and Decision-Making		Have the ability to make good decisions quickly
		Have the ability to solve problems
		Remove roadblocks inhibiting employees from getting things done
		Be responsible and competent
		Show good supervision, management, and leadership skills
7. Fair and Just		Provide equal treatment of all employees and fairness in all areas
		Act with objectivity and fairness
		Follow ethical guidelines
		Be consistent
		Judge employees solely on work performance
8. Honest and Trustworthy		Be honest, forthright, and transparent
		Be sincere, truthful, and trustworthy
		Act with integrity
		Be reliable
		Perform the work honestly

Appendix 2

Measuring Your ECM Competence with the ECM Scale

What are your capabilities as a people manager? Do you display competence on all eight ECM attributes, or just a few? How do your employees see you?

Once the eight-attribute taxonomy was created, these questions naturally followed. It is one thing to know and understand what employees want in a manager; it is another thing altogether to know how your employees see your performance in relation to these preferred attributes.

So, we need a measurement system that allows us to do that. Below is a brief description of the steps that were followed in the development process of the ECM scale:

Step One: Create the taxonomy. (See appendix 1)

Step Two: Draft or select a short list of items that allow employees to rate their manager on each taxonomy attribute.

Step Three: Complete an external review of the draft set of items by allowing well-informed others to compare my proposed items with theirs. This was accomplished by having five subject matter experts select their choices for measuring the eight attributes from a bank of items measuring a broad array of managerial behavior and performance. The comparison of their selections to my original list produced an overall agreement of 92%. Where there was not complete agreement on the best items to include, final decisions were made based on majority opinion. This process established the *content validity* of the proposed set of items or scale.

Step Four: Create a standardization sample by having typical respondents rate their managers on the items in the scale. This step was accomplished through a two-phase process. On two separate occasions over a two-year timeframe, a special survey of a representative sample of 5,000 workers in the United States was conducted; employees evaluated their managers on the items in the proposed scale. At the same time, employees were asked their attitudes about a variety of other topics, such as their current level of employee engagement, the interpersonal chemistry of their team, the overall effectiveness of their team, and so on. The two samples were independent and together provided a total sample size of 10,000 respondents. On both administrations of the survey, respondents were chosen to be representative of the total workforce in the United States as to industry, organization size, job type, job level, education level, age, and gender.

Step Five: Conduct psychometric analyses to determine the *internal consistency reliability* of the proposed scale. The resultant reliability coefficient was 0.96 out of 1, far exceeding the traditional standard threshold of 0.70 out of 1. In effect, this means the items in the scale are internally consistent; that is, they are measuring the same psychological construct, which in this case is the extent to which a manager is employee-centric.

Step Six: Conduct additional psychometric analyses to determine the ability of the scale to predict expected outcomes like overall managerial effectiveness. The results are presented in both chapter 1 and appendix 3. The analyses revealed that the scale is quite successful in predicting overall managerial effectiveness and other important outcomes such as EX (employee experience), employee engagement, team chemistry, and team performance. This verifies the *empirical validity* of the scale.

The steps outlined above are required to determine the appropriateness or scientific soundness of using a proposed scale as a valid and reliable means of measuring a psychological construct. The ECM scale meets all three major psychometric requirements: standardization, reliability, and validity.

As a result, we can use the scale below with confidence to measure the eight attributes contained in the ECM taxonomy. The scale contains 10 items. Two of the attributes—support and understanding and reward performance contributions—use two items apiece to measure the respective attribute. In terms of what employees most want from their manager, support and understanding was identified twice as often as the next most frequently identified attribute. This fact justified the use of two items to measure this attribute. As for reward performance contributions, this attribute clearly consists of two sub-attributes—one pertaining to rewarding performance through compensation and the other pertaining to rewarding performance with development opportunities. Given this, doubling the items allotted to this attribute was warranted. As a result, the overall ECM upward feedback measurement scale consists of 10 items:

1. **Support and understanding:** My manager is supportive of my coworkers and me.
2. **Support and understanding:** My manager is an effective listener.
3. **Recognition:** My manager provides me with recognition or praise for doing good work.
4. **Dignity and respect:** My manager treats me with dignity and respect.
5. **Clear performance expectations:** My manager communicates the performance expected of me.
6. **Reward performance contributions:** My manager does their best to ensure I am paid fairly for the work I do.
7. **Reward performance contributions:** My manager has made a personal investment in my growth and development.
8. **Problem-solving and decision-making:** My manager displays competence in making day-to-day work decisions.
9. **Fair and just:** My manager treats employees fairly.
10. **Honest and Trustworthy:** My manager is trustworthy.

To create actual measurements, the above items must be evaluated on a rating scale; the one used in this research is the *agreement scale* presented below:

1 = Strongly disagree

2 = Disagree

3 = Neither agree nor disagree

4 = Agree

5 = Strongly agree

This scale is known as a Likert-type rating scale, which is typical of those found in employee work attitude surveys.

This rating scale was chosen to make it easy to incorporate the 10 items of the ECM scale into a typical work attitude (e.g., employee engagement) survey. This allows the survey to provide, among other things, a readout of how employees view their managers on the ECM attributes. The core concept is that managers can use their results on the ECM scale items as a framework for development: strengthening themselves further on highly rated attributes and shoring up any attributes on which they were rated lower.

Now, the big question: How would your employees rate you on these 10 items? Are there some attributes on which your employees would rate you higher than average? Lower than average? Here are two facts: In the United States, considering all eight attributes, managers are rated highest, on average, on treating employees with dignity and respect and rated lowest on rewarding performance contributions. How about you?

As opposed to the scaling used in work attitude surveys, 180-degree (upward) and 360-degree performance feedback tools used for management assessment and development often employ a different rating scale, one that is based on the extent to which employees observe the display of a given attribute. Below is such a scale:

1 = To a very little extent

2 = To a little extent

3 = To some extent

4 = To a great extent

5 = To a very great extent

Psychometric research on the measurement of the ECM attributes on this *extent scale* produce virtually identical results to the research using the agreement scale typical of work attitude surveys. This means the ECM scale using the extent rating scale format also possesses high internal consistency reliability and strong empirical validity.

Appendix 3

Fuller Description of Research Summarized in Chapter 1

Chapter 1 presented nine reasons why you should read this book, digest its content, and apply its lessons. For those who want to dig a little deeper into my research, this appendix provides a fuller description of the methods used to arrive at my conclusions. I first restate the original reason and then provide my research support.

Reason 1: You want to better understand what employees most want from you

The truth is that most managers have only a partial understanding of what employees most want from them. That's right; most managers are limited in their grasp of the attributes of a manager that are most important to employees. How do I know this? I asked 1,000 people managers this question: "As a people manager, what do you believe is the most important thing your employees want from you?" I then compared their responses to the attributes employees said they most wanted in their immediate boss. The results appear below in Table A3.1, which is reproduced from Table 1.1.

Table A3.1

The Employee – Manager (Dis)Connection*

Managerial Attributes	What Employees Want	What Managers Think Employees Want**	Close Match?
Support and Understanding	25%	16%	No
Recognition	13%	1%	No
Dignity and Respect	13%	10%	Yes
Clear Performance Expectations	17%	15%	Yes
Reward Performance Contributions	7%	5%	Yes
Problem-Solving and Decision-Making	12%	19%	No
Fair and Just	8%	5%	No
Honest and Trustworthy	5%	13%	No

*Data based on samples from the United States
**Column totals to less than 100% because 16% of managers identified Overall Management and Leadership Skills as what employees most wanted from them

These results are specific to the United States, so the percentages in the first column of data do not perfectly match the global results. But that is not the point. The point of this table is to examine whether employees and managers value these attributes differently. To be sure, there are some close matches: dignity and respect, clear performance expectations, reward performance contributions, and even fair and just. The percentages of employees who indicate these four attributes are what they most want from their manager generally match the percentages provided by the managers themselves.

But look at two of the most frequently identified attributes: support and understanding and recognition. While more than one in four employees identified support and understanding as what they most want, only 16% of managers agreed. The comparison is most striking with recognition: 13% of employees identified this attribute as what they most want, while only 1% of managers thought the same. That is a very substantial difference and a clear miscalculation on the part of managers.

To round out the discussion, here are two final but less dramatic notes: managers generally overestimate the frequency with which employees state they most want their managers to be honest and trustworthy and competent in problem-solving and decision-making.

The bottom line: there are some people managers with a perfect or near-perfect understanding of what employees most want from them, but most managers have only a partial understanding at best.

Reason 2: You'd like to improve your capabilities as a people manager

Are managers getting the training and development they want and need to be good people managers? From the results of a recent survey of 1,000 people managers in the United States, this is what I learned:

- 71% indicated they had attended a formal management development training program with curriculum and study materials on the topic of people management; 29% had not.
- Of those who had attended such training:
  - 25% indicated their formal training totaled up to two hours
  - 36% indicated their formal training totaled between two and four hours
  - 39% indicated they had received more than four hours of formal training

What does this tell you? While it is somewhat reassuring that seven of ten people managers have received formal training in that role, it is dumbfounding that for three of five of those managers, formal training represented a time investment of no more than four hours.

Given the wide range of responsibilities inherent in managing others, does four hours of formal training in people management sound like enough to you? And remember, 29% of people managers have received no formal training at all.

These realities go a long way to explaining the clear desire for more training. I asked managers if they believed their capabilities as a people manager would improve because of formalized training or more formalized training on the topic of people management. 78% agreed, 18% indicated they were not sure, and only 4% disagreed.

It is not surprising that more than three-quarters of managers indicated a desire for more training. Again, for the 61% of those who had received training, it was capped at four hours. On a related note, almost one in five managers who had received a formal performance appraisal or review in the year indicated that the review made *no* contribution to the development of their people-management skills.

Talk about missed opportunities.

Training and development are about gaining knowledge, acquiring skills, changing behavior, and improving performance. By their own admission, most people managers in the United States are not getting the development they believe they need to improve their overall people-management capabilities.

Reason 3: Unknowingly, you overestimate your competence as a people manager

Some of the most influential leadership research states that what managers do boils down to two major behaviors. First, managers initiate structure; that is, they engage in helpful behaviors that facilitate the completion of their employees' work. This behavior has been shown to increase employee performance and productivity. Second, managers show consideration to employees; that is, they operate in a supportive, employee-centered way, which produces better supervisor-subordinate relationships and higher employee job satisfaction.

This historical research provides us with a starting point for measuring managerial performance. I supplemented measures of *initiating structure* and *consideration* with two overall measures of managerial performance to produce these four items:

- My manager does a good job of "managing the work": making appropriate work assignments, setting priorities, scheduling, and so on.
- My manager does a good job at "people management": dealing with the people who work for the manager.
- Overall, how effective is your immediate manager?
- My manager is an outstanding leader.

I first created an employee version of these items (above) and then created a managerial self-rating version of these items, with managers evaluating their own performance. For example, the manager self-rating version of the first item is: *I do a good job of at "managing the work": making appropriate work assignments, setting priorities, scheduling, and so on.*

I then obtained the ratings from 10,000 employees who evaluated the overall performance of their managers. The participating employees were representative of the workforce of the United States as to industry group, job type, age, gender, and so on. I also obtained self-ratings from 1,000 managers who evaluated their own overall performance. The participating managers were also representative of the managerial workforce in the United States. Extra care was taken to ensure a representative sampling of first-line, middle, and senior and executive managers. Table A3.2, which first appeared in chapter 1, shows the results of this research.

Table A3.2

Overall Managerial Effectiveness: Employee Ratings vs. Manager Self-Ratings

Elements of Overall Managerial Effectiveness	Employee Rating Average Score*	Manager Self-Rating Average Score*	Difference	Difference Statistically Significant?
Work Management	3.70	4.33	-0.63	Yes
People Management	3.67	4.30	-0.63	Yes
Overall Effectiveness	3.91	4.33	-0.42	Yes
Outstanding Leader	3.63	4.10	-0.47	Yes
Overall Average	**3.73**	**4.27**	**-0.54**	**Yes**

*Rating scale: 1 = lowest and 5 = highest score.

What do you see? On each of the four elements and on the overall average rating of managerial performance, managers rate themselves higher than their employees do. In fact, the differences are statistically significant. Granted, these are two different samples. The managers who rated themselves are not the same sample of managers that the employees were rating. But the fact that the samples are both representative of the US workforce and are sufficiently large makes the crucial point: Managers have an inflated view of their own performance compared to the views of employees.

Think of an analogy. When you purchase a product or service, it is not uncommon to be asked to complete a customer satisfaction survey. Those who produced the product or delivered the service no doubt have their own opinions of their work output. But in general, whose opinion is more important to the company providing the product or service? By far, it is the opinion of the customer. In a similar vein, whose evaluation is more important, the employees who are influenced (positively or negatively) by the features of their manager's behavior and style or the manager's?

In general, what this research project reveals is that managers tend to overestimate their own performance. It also reveals that if they listen to the real customers of their work—their employees—they will learn what they must do to become the manager their employees want: the employee-centric manager.

Reason 4: You'd like to create a superior work experience for employees

In the introduction, I define the employee-centric manager as the manager who displays the eight attributes that employees most want in their immediate boss.

Once the eight-attribute taxonomy was created, I devised a way of measuring the extent to which managers display these eight attributes (see appendix 2). Having the scores on the eight individual attributes allowed me to create an overall employee-centric manager score (ECM score). In technical terms, this is called a scale score, which is an overall summary of the extent to which managers display the eight attributes.

I then asked 10,000 employees to evaluate their managers using the employee-centric manager scale. Again, the participating employees were representative of the workforce of the United States in terms of industry group, job type, age, gender, and so on. This allowed me to identify leaders who scored in the top, middle, and bottom of the range on the employee-centric manager attributes. Top-rated managers are those scoring one standard deviation above the overall average ECM score, and bottom-rated managers are those scoring one standard deviation below the overall average ECM score. Those managers whose scores are within plus or minus one standard deviation of the overall average ECM score fall into the middle range.

Let's hit the pause button for a moment to discuss another topic, the employee experience (EX).

EX is a riff on the customer experience (CX). The importance of the CX in the design and development of new products is a given. Most organizations would not even consider new product development without considering the perspective of future customers, the very people who would pay for and use the product or service. After all, the new product or service is designed to address customer wants, needs, and expectations. When the CX is great, customers flock back for more of the product or service, purchase other products and services from the same organization, and tell their family and friends to do the same. A great CX is great for business in terms of customer loyalty, increasing sales, and market share growth.

So, it is only natural that this line of thinking has extended into the EX. Organizations have become increasingly concerned about creating an EX that will allow them to attract the talent they need, fully engage them, retain them, and even use them to advocate for the employer to bring in more top talent to fuel the organization's growth and success.

But how do we define EX? A summary of what has been written about EX tells us three things: 1) it is about designing the best possible experiences for employees, rather than making employees fit the organization; 2) it is a continuous process, rather than something that has an end goal; and 3) it can create engaged employees by focusing on the different aspects of the work experience, including culture, technology, and the physical workspace.

But if the idea behind EX is to build an appealing work experience for employees, shouldn't we ask what employees most want from their employer? Starting over 30 years ago, this is exactly what I have been doing. Back then, I did not call it EX, but I was asking employees to tell me, in their own words, how they define a great employer and how they describe a great work experience. I asked this question of over 300,000 employees from all over the world, representing all industries, job types, generational groups, educational levels, and genders. They told me a great EX includes the following components:

Recognition: A pat on the back—acknowledgment for a job well done—from managers and the organization.

Exciting Work: A job that is interesting, challenging, and fun.

Security: Confidence that solid work and a well-managed organization lead to job security.

Pay: Fair compensation for a day's work, meaning competitive pay and benefits: not always more, simply fair and reasonable in comparison to what employees bring to the job.

Education and career growth: Opportunities to develop skills over the course of a productive career.

Conditions: A well-equipped workplace that is physically comfortable but more importantly is socially inviting, inclusive, and team-oriented.

Truth: Frank, honest, and transparent communication from managers and senior leaders.

The first letters of these attributes form the acronym RESPECT. (This work is summarized in my book *RESPECT: Delivering Results by Giving Employees What They Really Want.*) With the taxonomy established, I devised a way to measure the RESPECT experience of employees. Fast forward and I now have RESPECT scale scores (which we'll call RESPECT EX scores below to use current terminology) for thousands of companies around the world. With that background, let's get to the point: how does the employee-centric manager influence EX?

To answer this question, let's go back to the employee-centric manager scale. Remember that I can characterize managers according to their ECM scores, which came from employees. Would it not follow that managers with higher ECM scores would also be the managers whose employees reported the highest RESPECT EX scores? In a nutshell, this is what I found:

- RESPECT EX scores of employees working for top-rated ECMs = 95%
- RESPECT EX scores of employees working for middle-rated ECMs = 70%
- RESPECT EX scores for employees working for bottom-rated ECMs = 21%

Here is the context. RESPECT EX scores can range from 0% to 100%, with average scores tending to fall in the 55%–65% favorable range. So, RESPECT EX scores for employees working for the top-rated ECMs do not merely dwarf the scores of those working for the bottom-rated ECMs, they exceed the all-industry average by 25 percentage points.

That is an enormous difference in EX. The employee-centric manager does indeed create a far superior work experience for employees. Those in the know about EX characterize it as the primary means to achieving the end of creating an engaged workforce. We look at that next.

Reason 5: You are interested in creating more engaged teams

We just demonstrated that the employee-centric manager has a powerful impact on EX. Specialists in EX tell us that it is the means to employee engagement, and in the past 20 years we have heard a lot about employee engagement. In fact, our science has evolved to the point where we can not only demonstrate that employee engagement is related to organizational performance, but also that employee engagement in fact drives organizational performance.

It sounds like we need to have a good understanding of employee engagement. What is it? Several years ago, we reviewed the literature on this construct and developed our own definition: "Employee engagement is the extent to which employees are motivated to contribute to organizational success and are willing to apply discretionary effort to accomplishing tasks important to the achievement of organizational goals."

Granted, that is a long sentence, but it boils down to this: Engaged employees are highly motivated, focused on important goals, and willing to apply discretionary effort. Past research shows that leaders and managers have a significant influence on employee engagement, so it stands to reason that employee-centric managers are not only going to impact EX but are also going to impact employee engagement.

How can we test this? First of all, we need to be able to measure employee engagement. I do this with five attitudinal items that are rated by employees. This produces an employee engagement index score:

- **Overall satisfaction:** Considering everything, I am satisfied with my organization as a place to work
- **Organizational pride:** I am proud to tell people I work for my organization.
- **Advocacy:** I would recommend my organization as a great place to work.
- **Commitment:** I intend to be working for my organization for a long time.

- **Discretionary effort:** My organization motivates people to work hard and to put in extra effort when needed.

So, when we measure employee engagement, we are picking up the perspectives of employees on their satisfaction, pride, advocacy, commitment, and discretionary effort. It is no wonder that employees who rate these attitudinal items favorably are more highly engaged employees.

We already know how to measure the extent to which managers are employee-centric. We have established that a strong positive relationship exists between a manager with a high ECM score and the EX of their subordinates. We have been told that EX is a means to employee engagement. It follows that employees working for top-rated employee-centric managers have higher employee engagement scores than those working for bottom-rated employee-centric managers. Here are the results:

- Engagement scores of employees working for top-rated ECMs = 97%
- Engagement scores of employees working for middle-rated ECMs = 76%
- Engagement scores of employees working for bottom-rated ECMs = 20%

As with RESPECT EX scores, employee engagement index scores can range from 0% to 100%. Recently, all-industry average scores have tended to fall in the 55%–65% favorable range. We are left with a similar conclusion: the employee engagement index scores of top-rated ECMs absolutely crush those of employees working for bottom-rated ECMs, and they outpace the all-industry average by 21 percentage points.

Now, we are connecting the dots. The managers who fulfill what employees want from them are the managers who help create a terrific EX and lead highly engaged teams. This follows naturally from the logic that EX is a means to high employee engagement. It also reinforces the outsized importance of the manager to both EX and engagement.

The story continues, with more dots to connect.

Reason 6: You're looking for ways to create a more positive and inclusive work environment

So far, we have focused on the individual employee outcomes of EX and employee engagement, and for good reason. The individual employee-individual manager relationship is key to employee satisfaction and commitment. But what about team outcomes? Do teams led by top-rated employee-centric managers enjoy better outcomes as well?

Let's start with team chemistry. Anyone who has worked on a team with lousy chemistry knows what a drag that can be—day after day with turmoil, agitation, and discontent. Employees come and go because voluntary resignations are high. It is not impossible of course, but certainly much harder for even the most talented employees to be at their best. They basically have to shut out what is going on around them in order to get their work done.

On the other hand, think about the best teams on which you have ever worked. How would you describe their chemistry? These teams have strong positive norms that regulate the behavior of members. These teams communicate well, and the high level of cooperation among team members supports team success. These teams are naturally cohesive and inclusive, and the inevitable conflicts that arise are not allowed to fester. Decision-making flows more quickly and successfully, and the confidence of team members is high.

Here are the employee work attitude items I use to measure team chemistry:

- **Inclusiveness:** I feel part of a team.
- **Cooperation:** The people I work with cooperate to get the job done.
- **Conflict resolution:** Conflicts within my team are resolved quickly and effectively.
- **Teamwork:** Where I work, teamwork is valued and encouraged.

The above items form the team chemistry scale. So, what is the relationship between employee-centric management and team chemistry? By now you know how this drill works. Let's see what happens when we compare team chemistry scores of those working for managers who are top-rated, middle-rated, and bottom-rated on the employee-centric manager scale.

Based on ratings of 10,000 managers, we learn the following:

- Team chemistry scores of employees working for top-rated ECMs = 99%
- Team chemistry scores of employees working for middle-rated ECMs = 75%

- Team chemistry scores of employees working for bottom-rated ECMs = 41%

The beat goes on. More dots become connected. The emerging story is supported not by simple intuition but by clear-cut empirical research. The research shows convincingly that those managers who deliver on employee preferences and expectations are managers whose employees enjoy great EX, high levels of engagement, and positive and inclusive team chemistry.

Reason 7: Achieving higher levels of team performance is a top priority for you

For at least the last 30 years, we have known (not surprisingly) that how employees describe certain aspects of their work environment correlates with descriptions provided by others. For example, consider the construct of customer satisfaction. How employees describe the emphasis at their place of work on customer service, anticipating and meeting customer needs, solving customer problems quickly, and so on almost always correlates positively and significantly with actual customer satisfaction survey results. In other words, how employees describe the service their team provides aligns with actual customer service ratings.

This demonstrates that employees are generally very well informed and, if asked the right questions, will shed considerable—and valuable—light on the efficiency of their workplace and what it will take to improve. This changes how we typically think about employee surveys. In addition to measuring EX and employee engagement, we can also use the perspective of the employee to diagnose what needs to be emphasized, changed, or completely overhauled to achieve better performance. The key point is that employees almost always know if their group is performing poorly, well, or somewhere in between.

It also means that we can typically predict the actual performance of a work team by asking members about the team's performance. The following items allow us to do just that:

- My work team is highly productive, getting the most out of our available resources.
- My work team produces high-quality work products or services.
- My work team consistently meets its goals on time.
- Overall, how effective is your work team?

This team performance scale gives us a solid reading on actual team performance. The question then becomes: Do teams that work for managers who deliver on the eight employee-centric manager attributes perform at higher levels than teams who work for managers who do not? Here is what I learned when I collected these data from a representative sample of employees in the United States:

- Team performance scores of employees working for top-rated ECMs = 99%
- Team performance scores of employees working for middle-rated ECMs = 75%
- Team performance scores of employees working for bottom-rated ECMs = 39%

Once again, we have a staggering difference for teams led by managers with differing employee-centric manager capabilities. To be sure, most teams rate their performance favorably—the national average for the United States is 76%. But even so, team performance for top-rated employee-centric managers beats the national average by 23 percentage points.

Whether we consider employee outcomes such as EX and engagement, or team outcomes such as chemistry and performance, the story is the same. Working for a top-rated employee-centric manager produces the best outcomes. And past research shows that all these employee attitude-based measures are in fact reliable predictors of actual business performance. All the dots connect.

Reason 8: You'd love to boost your overall managerial effectiveness ratings

A few decades ago, we saw the rise of 360-degree feedback systems as a way of providing more complete reviews on the performance of managers. The idea was based on the notion that, by including multiple perspectives (i.e., 360 degrees of feedback), a manager's performance review will be more valid, reliable, and useful to the manager. The multiple perspectives include not only the traditional top-down view from the manager's superior but also the views of peers, subordinates, and those outside the immediate workplace like customers, suppliers, and well-informed others.

A lot of research supported the use of these systems. A significant amount of research was focused on the idea of employees providing upward (or 180-degree) feedback. Some of the very best researchers in the field of industrial-organizational psychology concluded that the employee view was likely the most valid of all views because subordinates typically observed more of the manager's behavior and performance than anyone else. Additional research also documented that employee ratings of their manager's performance was positively and strongly correlated with ratings provided by that manager's manager.

As a result of this historical movement and the research supporting it, 360-degree and even 180-degree feedback systems are now common performance feedback and development tools used by larger employers in the United States and across the world.

How does all of this relate to the concept of the employee-centric manager? Earlier in this appendix (see Reason 3), I introduced a method of measuring a manager's overall performance that included two directly relevant items: one measuring overall effectiveness and the other measuring whether the manager is an outstanding leader. These two items, along with the two items that measure *consideration* and *initiating structure*, give us a very compact way of assessing the overall performance of managers. In appendix 2, I showed you how employees can rate their managers on the eight employee-centric manager attributes.

All of this is background to asking and answering this question: *Do employee ratings of managers on the eight employee-centric manager attributes correlate with or predict the overall performance ratings of managers*? If not, then we are left wondering how the employee-centric manager attributes relate to a manager's performance. More bluntly, we could then ask what the value of the employee-centric manager attributes is in helping us understand overall managerial performance. If, on the other hand, they do predict overall performance and that relationship is strong, we substantiate the importance of the eight attributes to the ratings of a manager's overall performance.

To determine whether the employee-centric manager attributes predict overall performance, we need data. I collected these data from over 10,000 employees in the United States over a two-year timeframe, ensuring that the data collection process produced a representative sample of US workers.

Using statistical regression analysis, here is what I learned: 67% of the variance (i.e., how spread out the dataset is) in the overall performance ratings of managers could be explained or accounted for by how subordinates rate their managers on the eight employee-centric manager attributes. Not all of us have a background in statistics, so what does this mean? It means that how an employee rates their manager on the eight employee-centric manager attributes determines or accounts for two-thirds of what goes into their overall rating of the manager's performance. **So, yes, how an employee sees you as a manager in terms of the eight employee-centric manager attributes largely determines how they see your overall performance.**

Said differently, if you are rated highly on the eight employee-centric manager attributes, you are almost guaranteed to be rated highly in terms of your overall performance. The reverse is also true; if you are rated poorly on the eight employee-centric manager attributes, it is almost impossible for your overall performance to be rated highly.

Scientifically, this is another step in building out the 5-1-2 theory of managerial effectiveness. But, practically speaking, you now know what determines whether your employees see you—in an overall sense—as an effective manager. Master the delivery or fulfillment of the eight employee-centric manager attributes, and you master your overall effectiveness as a manager from the perspective of your most important constituency: your employees.

Reason 9: You want an evidence-based pathway for your employee, team, and personal success

It is said a picture is worth a thousand words. I am not particularly good at drawing pictures, so how about a diagram? This diagram, reproduced from Figure 1.3, lays out my theory. A theory is simply an integrated set of principles that explains or predicts relevant outcomes. My theory starts with a universal taxonomy of what employees most want. It predicts what will happen for those managers who display these attributes in their interactions with their employees.

Figure A3.3

5-1-2 Theory of Managerial Effectiveness

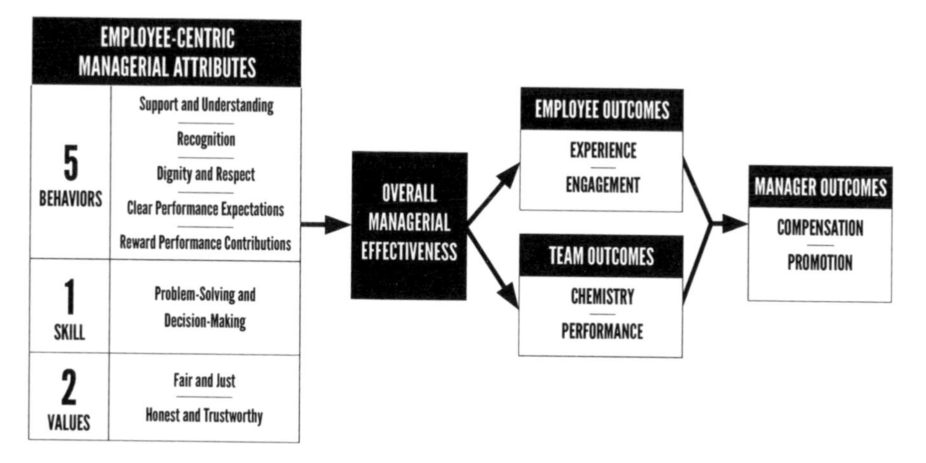

In words, the 5-1-2 theory of managerial effectiveness states:

There are eight universal attributes employees prefer in their managers. Behavior-wise, employees want managers who (1) show support and understanding, (2) provide recognition, (3) treat employees with dignity and respect, (4) communicate clear performance expectations, and (5) reward performance contributions. Skill-wise, employees prefer managers who are (1) competent in problem-solving and decision-making. Values-wise, employees want their managers to be: (1) fair and just, and (2) honest and trustworthy. Managers who demonstrate these attributes are seen by their employees as highly effective managers. Those who demonstrate these attributes contribute to a more favorable experience for employees and higher levels of employee engagement. Teams overseen by these managers enjoy better team chemistry and higher overall team performance. As a result, these managers gain higher compensation and greater promotional opportunities.

Everything presented is this book has a solid research base. The book does not relay any preconceived notions of mine. It simply lays out what I have learned by asking questions that are answerable by research. It describes the manager for whom employees aspire to work: the employee-centric manager. And it chronicles the positive influence that manager has on the attitudes and performance of their team members.

Appendix 4

Origin of Employee Sound-Off Comments

This book is based on asking employees to identify in their own words the attributes they most want in their managers. With the employee-based taxonomy of preferred managerial attributes established, it seemed only natural to return to employees to ask for examples of good (effective) and bad (ineffective) behavior of managers in relation to each of the eight ECM attributes.

This approach is called the *critical incident technique*, a research method formulated by John Flanagan, a highly respected industrial psychologist of an earlier generation. The use of this technique typically involves asking individuals to describe situations that depict good and bad (or effective and ineffective) displays of the behavior or attribute of interest. The basic idea is that collecting enough of these observations eventually enables a defensible drawing of general conclusions about the behavior or attribute.

This is how I used this technique for this book:

1. **Developing interview questions.** I developed questions to solicit both effective and ineffective examples of each of the eight attributes. Below are sample questions:

   Effective display of a manager being supportive: Think of a time when your manager did a great job of supporting you. Describe the situation: what the manager did, how it made you feel, and any long-term consequences to your relationship with your manager or organization.

Ineffective display of a manager being supportive: Think of a time when your manager did a lousy job of supporting you. Describe the situation: what the manager did, how it made you feel, and any long-term consequences to your relationship with your manager or organization.

Altogether, 20 such questions were prepared, 10 requesting positive displays of the attribute in question and 10 requesting negative displays. Four questions were devoted to the support and understanding attribute, with two devoted to each of support and understanding. As noted earlier, this attribute was identified as the one preferred by employees at least twice as frequently as any other attribute, so it warranted a broader investigation. Reward performance contributions also has two components: ensuring fair compensation and providing developmental opportunities. As a result, four questions were developed for this attribute to solicit effective and ineffective displays of each of its two components. Two questions apiece were devoted to all the other attributes.

2. **Drawing a representative sample.** A sample of 1,000 workers in the United States was drawn from a panel of survey respondents maintained by a global market research company. The sample was stratified to match the latest US Census statistics in terms of industry representation, job level, job type, education level, and gender. This was done to ensure that the collected data were representative of the United States workforce. All respondents

invited to complete the interview were at least 18 years of age. Other details regarding sample composition include:

- Respondents' average age: 42 years.
- Respondent composition by gender: 51% female, 49% male.
- Respondents came from a wide array of 21 industries, with the greatest representation coming from those in the health care services, high-tech manufacturing, retail trade, construction and engineering, government and public administration, banking services, and business services sectors.
- Respondent racial ethnic origin composition: 86% White, 9% African American, 3% Asian/Pacific Islander, and 3% Hispanic, which totals 101% due to rounding.
- Respondents represent all major job types, with the greatest representation coming from the professional, technical, clerical, sales, and laborer roles.
- Respondents represent all job levels: Individual Contributor (45%), Frontline Supervisor (10%), Mid-level Manager (29%), and Executive (15%).

3. **Conducting the online interview.** Given that there was a total of 20 questions and 1,000 respondents, each respondent was asked to answer only one question. This approach avoided respondent fatigue and promoted a high completion rate. All questions were preceded by a definition of the attribute participants were being asked about. An example is provided below:

Recognition. A manager who recognizes employees compliments and praises their good work, shows affirmation and appreciation, recognizes loyalty to the job and organization, recognizes both teams and individuals, and recognizes the efforts, passions, skills, abilities, and achievements of employees.

Interviewees typed their own response to the question posed to them.

4. **Selecting comments.** Approximately 50 respondents answered each question. Roughly 10%–15%, however, indicated that they could not produce or recall the type of requested incident. The selection of comments to include in the Employee Sound Off sections in chapters 3, 4, and 5 was based on how closely the comment related to the attribute under consideration and the extent to which comments offered unique information value. Several comments, even if they were expressed quite differently by different respondents, characterized the attribute in much the same way. When that occurred, the comments selected for inclusion in the book were those that were most readily understood. For each attribute, the goal was to present a variety of ideas by having the employees themselves describe good and bad managerial performance.

5. **Producing key takeaways.** The critical incident technique was designed to allow a researcher to draw supportable conclusions about the topic being investigated. In effect, the key takeaways presented in chapters 3, 4, and 5 represent my considered conclusions about how employees want their managers to display each of the eight employee-centric manager attributes.

The conclusions are naturally filtered through my own experience in both conducting research and in organizational life. All of the key takeaways are presented in the active tense as ideas managers can implement or maintain while on their employee-centric manager journey.

About The Author

Jack W. Wiley, PhD, is recognized internationally for pioneering research linking employee work attitudes to measures of organizational success. He is the author of two books published by Jossey-Bass, *Strategic Employee Surveys: Evidence-Based Guidelines for Driving Organizational Success* (2011) and *RESPECT: Delivering Results by Giving Employees What They Really Want* (2012).

Most recently, Dr. Wiley was professor of psychology for Manchester University where he founded the undergraduate program in industrial-organizational psychology. Prior to that, Dr. Wiley worked in business and industry for 35 years. After working for large corporations as an internal practitioner, he founded and served as CEO of Gantz Wiley Research, a consulting firm specializing in driving organizational success through the use of employee and customer surveys. Upon selling his practice to Kenexa, he founded and served as president of the Kenexa High Performance Institute. Dr. Wiley retired from IBM after its acquisition of Kenexa, but continues consulting with leadership teams around the world and serving as a keynote speaker at leadership events.

Dr. Wiley attended the University of Tennessee, earning a PhD in organizational psychology. He was elected Fellow of the American

Psychological Association, the Association for Psychological Science, and the Society for Industrial and Organizational Psychology (SIOP). Dr. Wiley received SIOP's lifetime achievement award for his distinguished contributions to professional practice. He is also a licensed consulting psychologist and accredited as a Senior Professional in Human Resources (SPHR) and as a SHRM Senior Certified Professional (SHRM-SCP).

Dr. Wiley currently serves as the Chief Scientific Officer at Engage2Excel and as the president and CEO of both Jack Wiley Consulting, LLC and Employee Centricity LLC.

Index

f following page number denotes figure; t following page number denotes table

D

E

F

G

H

I

N

O

P

Q

R

S

W